P9-CMA-275

Something Old Something New

701 Creative Ways to Personalize Your Wedding

by Becky Long

Meadowbrook Press

Distributed by Simon & Schuster

New York

Library of Congress Cataloging-in-Publication Data
Long, Becky.
    [From something olde to something new]
    Something old, something new : 701 ways to personalize your wedding /
by Becky Long.
        p.   cm.
    Originally published under title: From something olde to something new.
    Includes index.
    ISBN 0-88166-306-9 (Meadowbrook Press)
    ISBN 0-671-58126-0 (Simon & Schuster)
    1. Weddings—United States—Planning. 2. Wedding etiquette—United
States. I. Title.
    HQ745.L66   1997b
    395.2'2—dc21   97-42114
                                                          CIP

© 1997 by Becky Long

All rights reserved. No part of this book may be reproduced or transmitted
in any form or by any means, electronic or mechanical, including photo-
copying, recording, or using any information storage and retrieval system
without written permission from the publisher, except in the case of brief
quotations embodied in critical articles and reviews.

Cover Photograph: Maggie Merkow

Published by Meadowbrook Press, 5451 Smetana Drive, Minnetonka,
Minnesota 55343

BOOK TRADE DISTRIBUTION by Simon & Schuster, a division of Simon and
Schuster, Inc., 1230 Avenue of the Americas, New York, NY 10020

02 01 00 99 98   10 9 8 7 6 5 4 3 2

Printed in the United States of America

"To my mom and dad who gave
me the fairy-tale wedding I had
always dreamed of.
To my groom who made me realize
that fairy tales really do come true.
And to my son
for happily-ever-afters."

ACKNOWLEDGMENTS

I extend my thanks to the brides and grooms who shared their wedding days with me. To all of them, I send best wishes. Thanks also to the clergy and librarians who helped me discover forgotten wedding traditions. Likewise, I send salutations to all of the friendly folks from around the world who shared their wonderful wedding customs with me.

My special thanks go to Tim Lynch and Richelle Carlisle for design input, to Julie Day for illustrations, to Craig Holtzen and Kent Long for technical assistance, and to Stephanie Pinnell, Chuck McCann, and Renee Linnenkamp for their help in the initial launch of this project. I am also especially grateful to Bruce Lansky and the terrific staff at Meadowbrook Press for the creative energy and enthusiasm they have dedicated to the ongoing success of this book.

CONTENTS

Part 3: A Little Something Extra —— Checklists and Etiquette At-a-Glance

INTRODUCTION

He's popped the question and now it's time to start planning the rest of the fairy tale—your wedding day and the many activities that will occur during this special time in your life. To make a lasting impression, it is important that you find ways to personalize your celebration. Here at your fingertips you'll find hundreds of simple ways to help you do just that. From the ideas provided, you'll be able to incorporate those that you like best into your wedding festivities. The end result will be an occasion that's custom-fit to you and your groom.

Part I of this book offers unique ideas, including twists on tried-and-true wedding traditions. It's packed with creative solutions for all of your planning needs, whether you're looking for original invitations, decorations, favors for your guests, or gifts for your bridal party. Part II unveils wedding customs from the old world and around the world. There you may find a tradition that is symbolic of your heritage, your honeymoon destination, or one that has been almost forgotten, but shouldn't be. Part III makes this the complete wedding handbook. It could be dubbed the "saving" chapter as it offers time-savers, money-savers, headache-savers, and life-savers. In addition to suggested time lines and checklists, you'll find the rules that govern basic etiquette.

As you read on, remember that although most creative suggestions are listed only once to avoid redundancy, many can be introduced to your wedding planning strategy in a variety of ways. For example, an idea found under rehearsal dinner can also be incorporated into your wedding reception. In fact, to maximize the benefits from this book, you are encouraged to read each idea with this in mind. The goal of this book is to help you and your groom create wedding memories that will last a lifetime. Thus, let the fun begin...

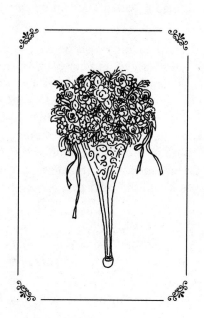

Something New

for

Something You

Original Wedding Concepts

Getting Started

To set the stage for an unprecedented nuptial celebration, you will need to stretch your imagination. In this section we'll energize your creative thought process by introducing novel theme wedding ideas featuring all the trimmings as well as innovative ideas for places to host your festivities. Our imaginative invitation concepts will pique your interest and that of your guests.

How to Make Your Brain Drizzle Instead of Fizzle (A Lesson in Brainstorming)

As a starting point to planning the wedding of your dreams, set up a file to help organize your ideas. You may want to establish separate files for categories including apparel, music, invitations, programs, reception, rehearsal dinner, flowers, photographer, videographer, church, and any other categories specific to your celebration. Include in your files pictures, magazine cut-outs, programs from other weddings, and any notes you may have written down.

Think big in your brainstorming; don't suffocate great ideas by assuming they're too expensive or too difficult to pull off. Research your options and then set a deadline after which prioritizing will begin. You may be surprised at how many of your dreams will come true in the end with the help of some shortcuts and minimal compromise.

Prepare to use your imagination. Here are some ideas to jump start your creativity.

- Curl up on the couch and watch videos of real life royal, presidential, or Hollywood weddings. You can always scale down to your budget some of the wonderful things that made these weddings so memorable. (Celebrities may not be able to offer the best marital advice, but they almost always know how to host beautiful weddings.)
  Hollywood classics for your review:

It Happened One Night 1934	*The Graduate 1967*
Gone with the Wind 1939	*The Godfather 1972*
The Philadelphia Story 1940	*A Wedding 1978*
Woman of the Year 1942	*Cousins 1989*
Father of the Bride 1950 and 1991	*True Love 1989*
High Society 1956	*Betsy's Wedding 1990*
The Catered Affair 1956	*Four Weddings and a Funeral 1994*
Funny Face 1957	

Royals to research:

Princess Elizabeth and Lt. Philip Mountbatten 1947
Grace Kelly and Prince Rainier III 1956
Hope Cooke and the Crown Prince Maharaj Kumar of Sikkim 1963
Lisa Halaby and King Hussein 1978
Lady Diana Spencer and Prince Charles 1981
Sarah Ferguson and Prince Andrew 1986
Masako Owada and Crown Prince Naruhito of Japan 1993

❧ Watch television. Commercials and daytime soaps could be two sources of inspiration.

❧ Window-shop at not just the obvious bridal salons, but also at candy, toy, and card stores. Who knows where you'll find the missing pieces to your wedding puzzle.

❧ Write away for free samples and catalogs. Bridal magazines are overflowing with ordering options.

❧ Comb craft stores and trade magazines. You'll be surprised at the clever one-of-a-kinds you can make, or buy if you feel you have two left thumbs when it comes to crafting.

❧ Visit the library or refer to the *Yellow Pages*.

❧ Browse through costume books and visit your local theater guild or costume shop for wedding themes. You may walk away with great ideas and also discover items for loan or rent. A visit to the first ladies' dress display at the Smithsonian in Washington, D.C., could also prove thought-provoking.

❧ Bounce creative ideas off of friends. While your tastes may differ, they may help you come up with neat ideas you never would have thought of on your own.

❧ Attend events such as Renaissance and ethnic festivals in your area. You may be able to get married there or hire some of their performers to appear at your special event.

❧ Turn to resources such as *Chase's Calendar of Events, Facts on File*, or a book entitled *On This Day* to learn about what happened on a particular day in history. Start with your wedding day and pick any year. Who knows where this information may take you. For example, if you're planning to marry on November 9, your wedding could take on a blackout theme as that's when lights went out in all of New York City in 1965. To keep your guests out of the dark, cleverly introduce the significance of the theme to them through the invitation, a cute sign, or a funny announcement.

Themes for the Wedding of Your Dreams

Picking a theme for your wedding activities can expand your creative possibilities. Your theme can encompass all of your planned festivities or it can be used, for example, at just the reception. Whatever the theme or themes, coordinating decorations and invitations will make your celebration more festive. Following is a sampling of ideas to get you started. Keep in mind you can use them as they are written or with modifications that are uniquely your own.

🔖 **Are either of you movie buffs?** If so, center your wedding celebration around Tinseltown. Set the stage by having a soloist sing a love song from a favorite movie at the wedding ceremony. At your reception, recreate a scene from your favorite movie and hire models to dress the part. Arrange for these scenes to "come to life" throughout the evening. The movie set can also inspire your food selections. For instance, if the movie is set on an island, then seafood would be a must. You can also name menu items after famous movie lines such as "Go Ahead, Make My Day" filet mignon and "Life Is Like A Box Of Chocolates" triple layer fudge. Request that waiters and bartenders dress as favorite cinema legends.

Likewise, give your guests the opportunity to say they sat with Robert Redford by using celebrity photos instead of table numbers. Or help them achieve celebrity status by leaving a pair of sunglasses at each place setting which could double as take-home party favors. Display table numbers or menu items on "action" clapboards. Tape individual place cards to favorite movie treats such as Junior Mints.

Show silent clips from favorite old movies on reel-to-reel projectors throughout the evening. Welcome guests with roving search lights and a marquee, and have entertainment reporters interview them upon their arrival. As bride and groom, enjoy the production center stage in director's chairs.

🔖 **Step back in time with all the romance and elegance of a Victorian wedding.** Begin by shopping for an antique engagement ring. (Unique ring styles are provided on pages 67–68.)

A vintage dress shop may have the perfect frock waiting for you. Or perhaps you could wear your great-grandmother's. If simple alterations cannot make that possible, maybe you could borrow a piece of lace from her gown and incorporate it into your bridal dress design, head piece, or bouquet. Crocheted gloves are a must for the Victorian bride, as is a top hat for the groom. Search for family heirlooms that will add something to your special day—perhaps a family Bible you could carry in lieu of a bouquet.

Arrange for each bridesmaid to carry a tussie-mussie. Tussie-mussies, popular with Victorian ladies, were elegant portable bud vases generally filled with nosegay bouquets of herbs and flowers (see illustration). Reproduction holders for tussie-mussies are widely available. For a long-lasting keepsake, fill tussie-mussies with dried flowers. (For the Victorian meanings assigned to various flowers and herbs, see pages 71–72.)

Parasols and picture hats are other accessory options from this period. Ribbon streamers tied in love knots will lend Victorian charm to candelabra and bouquets. In fact, the ribbons which streamed from Victorian grooms' boutonnieres were always elaborate and very long.

Invite guests to a Victorian-style mansion with a simple invitation adorned with pressed flowers or lace. Menus or name cards placed in small decorative Victorian frames will provide guests with a lasting treasure.

Say thanks to your bridesmaids with an antique hat pin holder or a locket. At your bridesmaids' luncheon, present each girl with an antique lace fan. Attach a note about the courting traditions which surrounded the fan during the Victorian era. (For more information on that, see page 66.)

For Victorian gift items or stationery, order the Victorian Papers catalog at (800) 800-6647.

🐜 **Your theme may also center around your honeymoon destination**. For example, if your plans will take you on a getaway to Italy, write parts or all of your invitation in Italian, being sure to include a translation. The invitation may also be trimmed in a beautiful Florentine design or adorned with golden cherubs.

To welcome guests to your reception, recruit people to pose as statues, reminiscent of the beautiful art of Italy. Also arrange for strolling musicians to serenade guests' tables with Italian love songs. Next treat your guests to a pasta bar while Italian beer and wine are served. And for another simple gesture that will translate into fun, consider piping Italian language tapes into your restrooms.

Cameos, which made their debut in Italy centuries ago, can serve as heirloom bridesmaids' gifts, while Italian leather belts will suit your groomsmen. (After all, you'll have their sizes from the tuxedo measurements.) Rely on an American-Italian tradition for your favors by letting guests take home bags of assorted traditional Italian cookies.

♣ **Invite your guests to dance the night away to the sounds of a big band.** Research clever song titles from that era. Design your invitation to look like song lyrics on a piece of sheet music.

Coordinate guests' tables to memorable tune titles. For example, guests sitting at Glenn Miller's "A String of Pearls" table will find not only sheet music as a part of the centerpiece, but also strands of pearls. Musical hits from this time will offer endless creative opportunities. Small musical instruments can be laced around table napkins. Luminaries with musical note cutouts can light up tables or the sidewalk that leads to your reception.

Serve up Count Basie's roast baron of beef and Frank Sinatra's bow-tie pasta. As bride and groom, pretend you're Ginger Rogers and Fred Astaire and show off the new steps you learned in a ballroom dance course.

♣ **Reap the benefits of a fall harvest wedding.** Design invitations in the shape of a leaf or have leaves embossed onto invitation envelopes.

Decorate your church or reception facility with teepees of corn surrounded by gourds of all shapes and sizes to create an autumn scene. Add lots of mums and apples spilling from bushel baskets. For your guest book or buffet table, create a leaf design on your tablecloth. (To make: Dip a real leaf or a leaf-shaped sponge into fabric paint. Press the paint-coated side of the leaf onto the tablecloth and remove without smudging for a special effect.)

Tablecloths in a rainbow of autumn hues will splatter dimensions of color throughout the dining room while cornucopias overflow with various breads. Use hollowed-out apples to hold votive candles for an especially festive look. Spiced apple cider will further complement your theme. Carved pumpkins surrounded by sprinkled candy or Indian corn would make a bright idea for centerpieces. Write guests' names on small gourds as an alternative to place cards. Tie wheat to each napkin. Make the dance floor appear to be in the middle of a pumpkin patch, with life-size bride and groom scarecrows.

♣ **Say *adios amigos* to boring wedding receptions with this idea.** If you and your groom met on *Cinco de Mayo*, then a Mexican theme would be entertaining and appropriate.

Set the mood by hiring a mariachi. Use minisombreros to hold the place cards for your sit-down dinner, with larger sombreros filled to the brim with wildflowers at the center of each table. Uniquely-painted terra cotta pots can serve as delightful favors, especially if they hold a cactus for each guest. Mexican pottery or rugs will give your bridal party members something to remember you by. After cutting the cake, it will be time for the bride and groom to bust the piñata. Curb hungry appetites with chips and salsa at each table. Margaritas will also be a menu must.

You could also elope to Mexico and host this reception upon your return. Whatever the case, no guest will get caught taking a siesta at your fun-filled reception.

🌢 **Up, up, and away is where this theme can take your wedding planning inspirations.** Fill your hotel ballroom with balloon archways and string a confetti-filled balloon to each chair. Arrange for a balloon drop during the bride and groom's first dance. Tickle children and adults alike with the addition of a balloon artist to twist balloons into a variety of shapes.

Top off your buffet table with a cake that's made to look like a hot-air balloon. Recreate the famous hot-air balloon scene from *The Wizard of Oz* as a backdrop to your festivities. For the grand finale, say farewell to your guests as you make your get-away via a hot-air balloon.

🌢 **If your romance has read like a fairy tale you may want to consider playing out that theme.** Begin your invitation copy with a very fancy uppercase letter and end with the phrase "and they plan to live happily ever after." Give each of your guests an inexpensive copy of your favorite fairy tale with a personal note as a favor. Or hire someone to write a personalized fairy tale of your courtship, complete with illustrations. Make the story come to life with a professional storyteller.

Exit the church in a horse-drawn carriage. Create an indoor pond with a frog on a lily pad as the focal point for your decorations. A sign next to the frog could read "You have to kiss a lot of frogs before you find your prince." Likewise, a visit from a fairy godmother granting wishes will make the fairy tale complete. The many wonderful tales in circulation will offer endless musical selections to which you can dance the night away. Favorite animated fairy tales can play on small screens throughout the reception—while your real life fairy tale unfolds.

🌢 **A Renaissance wedding will take your guests back in time.** Ask that they come in costume and hold your affair at an art museum. Dress your flower girl in a wreath made of dried roses and ribbons while the ring bearer carries a velvet pillow. Choose velvet and satin bridesmaids' dresses.

Incorporate elegant tapestries in deep, rich colors to run the length of your buffet table. Trim with floral swags and fruit garlands. Surprise guests with giant turkey drumsticks served on china plates. Feature renditions of Michelangelo and Raphael's works of art on invitations, centerpieces, cakes, or ice sculptures. Decorate chair backs with velvet bows and napkins with tassels.

🐾 Tie the knot where ropin' is a way of life by getting hitched on a ranch. Find a remote cabin somewhere or create your own chapel in the middle of nowhere with hay bales for pews. Your bouquet of freshly picked wildflowers will make for beautiful pictures.

To make it a real showdown, plan for the entire bridal party to wear cowboy boots. Travel horseback to your reception where a bar in the back of a covered wagon awaits. After guests two-step the night away, send them home with a bandanna full of surprises. Give groomsmen branding irons with their initials so your gift will be put to good use at backyard barbecues for years to come. For more information write to Sloan Brands at Route 3, Box 22B, Hico, TX 76457.

🐾 Set sail with your guests without really going anywhere. Print your invitations in the shape of a boat to welcome folks aboard the "S.S. Honeymoon." Dress small children in the wedding party in sailor suits and have them carry sand buckets instead of flower baskets.

Carry out the theme by stringing lights in the shape of a cruise ship on the front of your reception hall. Have servers don nautical attire while serving up coconut shrimp, fruity drinks in pineapples, and swordfish on a stick. Whet your guests' appetites with a succulent seafood buffet where an ice sculpture of a dolphin will fish for compliments. Serve up shrimp in plastic toy boats. Name tables after various creatures of the sea. Draw the "sea"ting chart to resemble an underwater view of the ocean, showing, for example, where the octopus, shark, and whale tables are located. Decorate the room with buoys and fish nets draped with beautiful seashells. Use international sailing flags and pennants to spell out the bride and groom's names in decorations or on print materials. Add topiaries made of seashells to each table. Use raffia to tie seashells to place cards or folded napkins. Create a top-deck feel by stringing little white lights overhead to make a starry night come to life.

Make sure your DJ or band is equipped with lots of songs about the sea and sailing. A boat horn will get the group's attention for the toast while helping to set the mood. Guests can say bon voyage to the bride and groom with streams of confetti.

Leave a fishing lure at each place setting with a note attached that says, "Michelle fell for Craig hook, line, and sinker on September 10, 1996." Or send guests home with sand dollar ornaments. (To make: Tie ribbon through sand dollar, glue on smaller shells, and add your names and wedding date.)

If you're not leaving right away on your honeymoon, a bon voyage brunch might give you a chance to catch up with all of your out-of-town guests.

ও **Jingle bells and wedding bells make a superb combination.** One of the perks to having a holiday wedding is that many churches already have a bountiful supply of decorations, so you'll save on that line item of your wedding budget without compromise. With a holiday theme wedding, you could go with the traditional colors of red and green. Or perhaps you're dreaming of a white wedding. Regardless, a bell prelude or a children's choir performing traditional songs of the season would be a wonderful way to set the stage for your ceremony. Your bridesmaids could carry lanterns adorned with sprigs of holly.

Work with your florist to create a winter wonderland at your reception complete with angels, loads of evergreen, and snowflakes. If weather permits, recruit some children to build bride and groom snow people in front of your reception facility to welcome guests. Make your dance floor look like a picture-perfect ice-skating pond with mistletoe above. Dress doors as giant packages and transform white columns into larger-than-life candy canes by wrapping them in red tulle. Recruit a ballet class to perform a selection from *The Nutcracker.*

Play holiday classics with no sound in the background. If *It's a Wonderful Life* is one of your favorites, then attach a bell to each place card that reads "Every time a bell rings, an angel gets his wings." At each place setting, make the plate "present"able by tying it up with a big bow (see illustration). Tie sprigs of holly around each napkin and stuff silverware into small mittens or stockings. For table centerpieces, consider gingerbread houses. Edible gingerbread men place cards might also be a nice touch.

For favors, give each guest a bell or an elf hat, or both. Think about how festive it would be to make your getaway through a tunnel of Santa's helpers ringing bells. Attach a personalized ribbon and consider having your favors personally delivered to each of your guests by jolly old St. Nick himself. Serve finger sandwiches and cheese cut into shapes of the holiday season along with eggnog. Slide out of sight on a sleigh with the man in red at the reins.

🐦 **If you're planning to wed during the winter months in a cold climate, think about delighting your guests with an indoor garden party**. Begin by literally dressing your flower girl as a flower.

Continue the theme at the reception with a maypole in the center of the room surrounded by potted tulips. Serve up salad with garden spades and fresh bread in terra cotta pots. Decorate mints with a variety of iced edible flowers. (See page 31 for a listing of edible flower varieties).

Place items such as watering cans, garden gloves, bunnies, and stemmed carrots throughout your reception area. For breathtaking focal points consider garden statues, fountains, or a gazebo drenched in flowers. Find an assortment of colorful birdhouses to perch at the center of each table. In addition, send guests home with birdseed favors. (To make: Drill a small hole into the top of a thin wood form. Spread nontoxic glue over form, then roll the form in birdseed until covered. Thread ribbon through the hole at top and tie to form loop for hanging. Attach a note saying "Remember to feed the birds this winter." Wood forms are available in all shapes and sizes.)

Say thanks to bridal party members by giving each a set of gardening tools or a rose bush in your wedding colors. Invite guests to watch your love grow by sending a packet of flower seeds with your invitations to be planted in honor of the newlyweds. The front of these invitations could feature a pressed wildflower. Or order plantable invitations from Bloomin' Flower Cards at (800) 894-9185. The handmade paper jackets of these custom-designed invitations are embedded with wildflower seeds which guests can plant following the wedding.

🐦 **Give your formal wedding a real twist by suggesting that your guests wear creative black-tie apparel.** For example, if you and your groom are avid tennis players, list the dress as a combination of black tux and tennis togs.

Use tennis jargon in bold print throughout the invitation copy. For example, "Brenda and Todd first **courted** and are now the perfect **match.** Their **score** will forever be **love-love**." Send invitations in empty tennis cans.

Hold the reception on a tennis court and feature food stations that serve up entrees representing the countries where big matches such as Wimbledon and the French Open are held. Welcome guests with wreaths made of tennis balls. For centerpieces, fill bright colored gym bags with flower arrangements.

🐾 Transport the revelry from medieval days to modern day by hosting a Camelot wedding that's fit for a king and queen. Announce your royal affair by adding your family coat of arms to your invitation written in calligraphy. Direct the bride and groom's families to the appropriate sides of the church with shields bearing each family's crest.

Welcome guests to the reception with juggling jesters, strolling minstrels, and a knight in shining armor. Request that your bartender dress like Merlin the magician. Seat attending "knights" at nothing but round tables. Precede guests' names on place cards with Lord or Lady. The signs on the restroom doors could reflect the same. Enlist heralds to proclaim your arrival as bride and groom with banners and horns.

Spear hors d'oeuvres with tiny swords. Likewise, award each table centerpiece to the person who finds the paper Excalibur sword taped to the bottom of his chair. Use a sword to cut the first slice of your castle-shaped wedding cake. With final fanfare, make your getaway on horseback.

For the rehearsal, stage a pig roast the night before, but pretend it's wild boar. Thank groomsmen with chess sets or something bearing each attendant's coat of arms.

🐾 If you and your groom are wine connoisseurs, offer a wine tasting at your reception. Adorn the entry way to your reception with a grapevine trellis. Use large decorated grapevine wreaths for table centerpieces and mini ones as napkin rings. Display each place card in a sliced wine bottle cork. Inspired by the theme, hunter green and burgundy would be marvelous color choices.

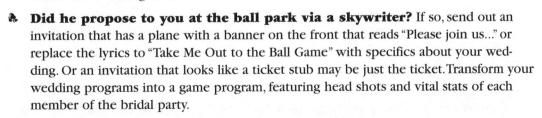

Design your invitation copy to read like a wine label. For favors, create personalized label stickers to decorate miniature wine bottles (see illustration). Or call Private Cellars at (800) 800-4436 to order imported gold bottles of champagne with labels that feature your names and wedding date.

🐾 Did he propose to you at the ball park via a skywriter? If so, send out an invitation that has a plane with a banner on the front that reads "Please join us..." or replace the lyrics to "Take Me Out to the Ball Game" with specifics about your wedding. Or an invitation that looks like a ticket stub may be just the ticket. Transform your wedding programs into a game program, featuring head shots and vital stats of each member of the bridal party.

Maybe you would like to say "I do" on home plate of your favorite baseball diamond or host your reception on the same field where your husband played little league. Or take the celebration indoors and create a similar atmosphere by laying an artificial-turf dance floor with bases in each of the four corners. Green tablecloths decorated with white crepe paper baselines will further your theme.

Have bartenders dress in umpire uniforms while waiters dress as vendors, complete with hanging trays to serve up popcorn, peanuts, cotton candy, and Cracker Jack. Line up traditional ballpark organ music to be played as the first pitch of bouquet and garter are thrown. Ask the band leader, who will act as an announcer through these important festivities, to sport a sportscaster jacket and microphone.

Centerpieces can rest in ball caps or gloves. Decorate each table in different professional team colors and invite guests to sit with those teams. If your party's a hit, fans may do the real wave as the bride and groom run off the dance-field.

Design thank-you notes to resemble baseball trading cards, featuring a picture of the bride and groom complete with wedding stats.

Plan a New Year's Eve wedding. It will provide you with ready-made plans for this important holiday every year and many festive decorating opportunities. You may even save money on decorating costs, as many facilities will still be dressed for the holiday season.

Invite guests to ring in the New Year with you by stringing bells onto invitation corners. Begin your service with a performance by a bell choir.

Let "Auld Lang Syne" serve as the audio backdrop for a slide show of your youth. Tie small strands of bells around the stems of guests' toasting glasses. Make it a black-tie affair. Using the traditional New Year's colors of black and white, find penguins of different shapes and sizes to use in your decorations. To the real-life penguins, otherwise known as groomsmen, add top hats.

A giant clock could be the perfect backdrop for your band or DJ. Of course, make sure you include some of the expected streamers and noisemakers. Use personalized party hats for place cards.

Hire a fortuneteller to roam the crowd, making new year predictions for each of your guests. Plan carefully for the stroke of midnight to make it a New Year's celebration that rivals Times Square. Some inspiring ideas might include a balloon drop from the ceiling, bubble machines, or the drop of a big papier-mâché wedding bell. Send each guest home with a calendar for the new year.

🐾 **And finally, let's plant yet another idea for a theme wedding by centering your celebration around the family tree.** Feature your individual family trees on the invitation cover. Inside show a new branch beginning to form with a verse about your love growing for one another. Mail tree seedlings with invitations. To order seedlings, call The Greenworld Project at (800) 825-5122.

Add beautiful handmade paper covers to wedding programs. Attach the cover to your program with the help of a hole punch, a small branch, and raffia (see illustration). Add dried petals to your paper mixture from flowers the groom sent to you in the past and make note of that inside the program. Glue a pressed leaf onto the program's front. (Paper-making kits are available at most craft stores or see page 51 on how to order.)

To top off this theme, consider marrying in a beautiful park or family garden. Plant a tree to dedicate your love to one another.

Now that you're warmed up, let's explore some additional ideas.

🐾 **The Wizard of Oz** - Dress bridesmaids in the colors of the rainbow. To add a magical element, add ruby red slippers to your bridal attire. Lead guests to the dance floor with a yellow brick road. Make it appear as if the buffet table landed on the wicked witch by having her feet stick out from under the tablecloth. Use poppies in table centerpieces while place cards rest on miniature scarecrows. Start the reception with someone dressed as the mayor of Munchkinland to read a proclamation of marriage. Beg your groomsmen to perform a number as the Lollipop Guild.

🐾 **Jungle** - Place an abundance of large potted plants and exotic flowers just inside the front doors to your reception hall to create a jungle effect. As your guests move through the thicket, they'll feel like they are going on an African safari. Consider having a large elephant or giraffe made of cardboard greet them in the clearing. Some jungle sound effects would bring your decorations to life. Ask your emcee and bartenders to wear safari-guide attire.

🐾 **Old South** - Request that ladies dress as belles in hoop skirts and that men wear military uniforms. Marry on the lawn of a beautiful old Southern mansion where a cannon can be seen in the distance. Arrange for a 21-gun salute upon your announcement as husband and wife. Give guests a real taste of the Old South by serving mint juleps.

- **Calling All Bookworms** - If you and your husband are both book enthusiasts, consider a library as your reception venue. Use the Dewey decimal system to develop your seating chart and send your guests home with a bookmark which features a quotation such as Abraham Cowley's "May I a small house and large garden have; and a few friends, and many books, both true, both wise, and both delightful too!"

- **Halloween** - For the wedding that occurs during the haunting season, consider treating your guests to a masquerade ball. To decorate, use a variety of trick-or-treat bags to make each table centerpiece unique. Incorporate carved pumpkins into your buffet table design or use them to line the dance floor. Change solid white napkins into ghosts at each place setting. (To make: Stuff the napkin into a glass and add black dot sticker eyes.) Write guests' names on small masks and use as place cards. The conservative approach to this theme might allow for the groomsmen to wear orange cummerbunds.

- **Valentine's Day** - Design your wedding invitations to look like the kind of valentines you exchanged in the second grade. Hire Cupid to pay a visit to your reception, and make sure he brings his bow and arrow. Topiaries in the shapes of hearts can adorn each table along with scattered rose petals. Serve up heart-shaped scones. Send your guests home with wedding cake in heart-shaped boxes.

- **St. Patrick's Day** - The question is simply how much green do you want to see. Some traditions include corn beef and hash, shamrocks, green beer, and pots of gold. Your ring bearer may also double as a leprechaun.

- **Fourth of July** - Start with a patriotic color scheme. When you're announced as husband and wife, arrange for a parade of fireworks to light the sky. (Check out local fireworks regulations.) Roll napkins to look like firecrackers and stuff gold confetti in napkin top to resemble flame. The napkin ring can look like a firecracker label, but serve as a take-home keepsake when you add the bride and groom's names and wedding date. Top wedding cake with sparklers. Treat the signing of your marriage license like the signing of the Declaration of Independence.

- **The Homecoming Wedding** - This theme can be the perfect solution if both families live far away. Elope or stage a very intimate affair to say your actual vows, then travel to both of your hometowns for subsequent celebrations.

    Another spin on this theme would be appropriate if you are marrying your high-school or college sweetheart. Travel back to your alma mater where the romance began and get married in the school gym or chapel. Create an invitation resembling a graduation announcement with a picture of the school on the front (see illustration).

Instead of including individual name cards that are traditionally found in graduation announcements, write both of your names together on one with the following at-home information:

Mr. and Mrs. Douglas Day
at home
after the first of January
555 West Mississippi Street
Bentonville, KS 55555

Use school colors as wedding colors. Welcome each lady with a large homecoming mum. Remember to invite the school mascot.

- **The Honeymooners** - Invite guests to your wedding and on your honeymoon as well. Meet for an extended stay in mountain cabins or thatch huts along the beach. Or embark on a cruise through the Orient. (Research pertinent marriage laws. If your nuptial destination is in another country, then plan ahead as there could be lots of red tape.)

- **The Reunion** - Make it an extended weekend where spending quality time together is the focus. Plan several informal parties such as golf matches, barbecues, picnics, relays, and softball games. For competitive sporting matchups, you may want to have T-shirts or cups printed.

- **Roaring 20's** - In honor of Prohibition, feature beer made at a local brewery. Inquire about renting out their facility at a time when they are generally closed to the public. To keep in theme, give groomsmen personalized beer steins. Teach everyone to do the Charleston, a dance that became especially popular at this time.

- **Elizabethan** - Feature favorite excerpts from Shakespeare's sonnets or perhaps a simple quotation on your wedding invitation. One to consider from *Romeo and Juliet* is "My bounty is as boundless as the sea, my love as deep; the more I give to thee, the more I have, for both are infinite." Design the wedding program like an old-world playbill. To further carry out this dramatic theme, have Puck, a mischievous fairy from *A Midsummer Night's Dream,* greet guests. And finally, invite guests to be seated at tables named after characters such as Hamlet, Macbeth, and King Lear.

🐾 **Surprise** - If you want to catch your guests by surprise, invite them to a birthday party which turns into a wedding.

*L*ocation, Location, Location

The venues you select for your festivities will set the tone for your entire celebration. We've highlighted some out-of-the-ordinary possibilities.

🐾 Consider the zoo, an ice-skating rink, a rose garden, art gallery, airplane hangar, aquarium, barn, ranch, apple orchard, miniature golf course, greenhouse, lighthouse, winery, wine cellar, vineyard, brewery, paddleboat, yacht, cave, mansion, museum, gym, theater stage, playground, town square, stadium, ski lodge, a clearing in the woods, a hilltop, or an open field of flowers. (Pick a location like one of these and you won't have to worry about bumping into another bride in the ladies room.)

🐾 Check with the historical society in your area. You may find a wealth of information from local history buffs.

🐾 Reserve an old monastery as the site for your period wedding.

🐾 Remember there's no place like home. There's always your own back yard. (However, don't assume this will also be your least expensive option, as importing amenities can be costly.)

🐾 Make it a getaway wedding. Head to Key West and say "I do" on Malory Square just before sunset. A sunset celebration of great magnitude is sure to ensue in this tropical paradise. Or if parkas are more your style, travel to the mountains of Colorado and say your vows at the top of your favorite ski slope. Two other getaway options include marrying at a theme park or on a cruise. Keep in mind that you don't always have to travel far from home to feel as if you've escaped. Consider retreating to a vacated Boy Scout or church camp.

🐾 Be creative. Waterfront locations are always popular, especially on America's coastlines. Take the plunge on board a yacht and have guests follow you through the harbor in a parade of boats.

🐾 If you find yourself landlocked in the Midwest, remember that you can marry on a riverboat cruise, pool-side, lake-side, fountain-side, or in front of a cascading waterfall in a beautiful hotel lobby.

🐾 Inquire about hosting your afternoon wedding reception at a bar or night club that is not normally open during the day. They may not even think of themselves as being in the wedding business but may welcome the invitation.

♣ Revisit a favorite family vacation spot or the place where the two of you met or became engaged.

Be a Pioneer on the Paper Trail (One-of-a-Kind Invites, Programs, and More)

You will make an important first impression on your wedding guests with the invitation you send. Your other print materials will also become cherished keepsakes.

♣ Personalize your invitations by starting with your baby photos, then add a favorite quotation or Bible verse. Or use your baby footprints and talk about how first you learned to walk alone, but now the two of you will walk together. If you are an artist or know an artist, add a favorite sketch to the front or draw a series of sketches and have your guests flip through it quickly to set the pictures into motion. Perhaps a watercolor drawing is something you have always pictured. Your local print shop can also help you develop something from scratch. Here's an example:

Yesterday is today's memory...

REBECCA

·Curtis·

(Inside)

Tomorrow is today's dream.
As friends and family you've
shared many special memories
with us in the past.
Please join us as we unite our
dreams for the future on...

Sometimes the cost of personalizing invitations is only pennies more than the printing costs of more traditional invitations.

♣ Reflect your heritage on your invitation. If you're Irish, you might want to put a Claddagh on the front, a design featuring two hands holding a heart topped with a crown. The Claddagh symbolizes love, friendship, and loyalty (see illustration).

♣ Find a newspaper article or cartoon that sums up your relationship or the occasion and simply change the headline. Use it in any of your print materials from invitations to thank-you notes.

♣ For one-of-a-kind invitations, consider adding a unique hand-painted trim to your preprinted invitations.

♣ Explore different fonts as well as unique colors and textures of paper. To order a book of paper samples from around the world, call Paper Source at (800) 248-8035.

- Visit an old-time photo shop where you dress in costume and have your picture taken. Add the end result to the front of your invitations or programs for a period wedding.

- Use the flower girl's rendition of the bride and groom as the artwork for sentimental invitations, programs, or thank-you notes. Make sure you give proper credit. A professional caricature is another option.

- Remember that any blank cards with a pretty picture or design on the front will work for your invitations. Party details can be printed on the inside.

- Skim through classic poetry from philosopher Kahlil Gibran in *The Prophet* for the perfect sentiment for your personalized invitations or programs.

- Learn calligraphy or find someone for hire to address your wedding invitations. It's a very classy touch to a formal invitation.

- Include maps to every wedding activity. They are especially helpful for your out-of-town guests. A cartoon version might make the drive a little more enjoyable (see illustration).

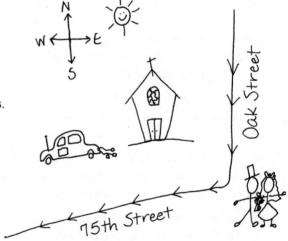

- Create entertaining wedding programs. If you are a print journalist and the groom is in advertising, design your program like a newspaper. If you're into theater, a playbill would be a unique format. Programs can feature a poem or favorite cartoon that is special to the bride and groom. They will also serve as marvelous mementos from your wedding if they feature a tear-off bookmark and a special note. Include pictures of all of the bridal party members from years past, ideally at play with the bride or groom. Add to that a paragraph about how the friendship began, and you have interesting preceremony reading material (see illustration next page).

Your programs might also include your new address, thank-you's, and instructions if, for example, you will be ushering guests out after the ceremony. On the same note, the program can be the ideal place to explain the symbolic meaning behind other special touches you may have incorporated into your ceremony. For instance, you may want to include the lyrics to a song that was written especially for you and your groom and performed during the ceremony.

"As brothers, this was the only time Mom and Dad could get them together where they were clean, smiling, and not punching each other. Today you will see them clean and smiling."

Childhood picture of groom with younger brother, a groomsman

🐾 Ask a special friend or relative to serve as a program boy or girl so that your guests will be sure to get a program.

🐾 Keep everyone up to date on tuxedo rental, hotel reservations, dress fittings, and start times with an amusing newsletter. The newsletter could be accompanied by luggage tags to surprise out-of-town guests. With the initial mailing of your newsletter, also include information from your local chamber of commerce to assist those guests who may want to vacation in your area after the wedding. Include items such as a map of the city, schedules of local sports teams and museums, plus a calendar of events. A brief bio and picture of each of your bridal party members may also help them become better acquainted with each other.

🐾 In addition to keeping your family and friends informed, keep the world abreast of your wedding matters by putting a wedding home page on the Internet. There guests may accept your reception invitation, check bridal registry, or even download a video broadcast of your ceremony.

🐾 Include a candid or professional picture of the bride and groom in wedding attire on the wedding thank-you notes. To save precious time, use note cards featuring die-cut slots into which you can later slip a photograph so that you can begin writing your thank-you's while your pictures are being developed.

🐾 Arrange to have a black and white photo taken of you and the groom in everyday clothes, only he should wear a top hat and you, a veil. Use this on the front of your thank-you notes with copy that reads "As bride and groom we're starting to get settled in, but first we wanted to thank you." Remember to include a handwritten thank-you as well.

- Hide confetti in invitation envelopes. Try foil wedding bells or hearts.

- Hire someone to dress in a tuxedo and white gloves to hand-deliver each of your in-town invitations for a small, formal wedding.

- Incorporate your wedding theme into your postage stamps. There are always the obvious "love" stamps. Today, however, the post office has even more to offer in this department with commemorative stamps that feature everything from fish to western motifs to movie stars.

- Order extras of everything for future use at an anniversary party.

- Ask a friend to mail one of your invitations to you on your wedding day so you'll have your wedding date postmarked on the envelope as a keepsake.

- Send one or all of your invitations to Loveville, Maryland. They have developed a special postmark for weddings and anniversaries. Just send your box of stamped and addressed invitations to the Postmaster's attention in Loveville, MD 20656. Include a brief note of instruction. Once postmarked, the invitations will then be sent from Loveville to your guests. If it's just one invitation envelope you want postmarked for the scrapbook, send it enclosed in another envelope to the same address given above. Also include an envelope with return postage so that your original invitation envelope can be returned to you without picking up other postmarks along the way. Depending upon the number of postmarks you are requesting, there may be a nominal charge. Call Loveville's post office at (301) 475-5243 for more information.

Loveville, Maryland
20656

Creating an Affair to Remember

You don't have to be movie stars like Cary Grant and Deborah Kerr to make your wedding *An Affair to Remember*. Instead, there are simple ideas you can incorporate into your ceremony and reception to keep guests talking about your wedding for years to come.

You Don't Need to Decorate the Steeple to Wow the People

Your church decorations will set the ambiance for your ceremony. Whether formal or informal, sometimes simple is best. As you explore your decorating options, consider the time of day your wedding will take place as well as the church's permanent decor. Keep in mind that candles will not have the same impact during a daytime wedding as they will at night. If you want to use fresh flowers outside the church, you'll also have to take the temperature and weather into account. For an outdoor wedding, analyze ways you can capitalize on the landscape.

As you begin planning your decorations, establish a focal point. From there, surround yourself in whatever makes you most comfortable. While there are endless possibilities, we've highlighted some favorites.

- Welcome guests to the church by placing a seasonal wreath on the front door. Consider bittersweet in the fall, evergreen in the winter, and sunflowers in the spring or summer.

- Dress tree trunks outside the church with big satin bows.

- Place a pair of blue spruce trees on the front steps of the church. Add panache with strands of white lights and ribbon bows in wedding colors.

- Greet guests with fragrant flowers as soon as they walk into the church. Consider an arrangement of gardenias or a single bloom placed in a shallow dish of water at the guest book table.

- Gather swags of greenery on church railings. Adorn with giant bells or fruit clusters.

- For an autumn wedding, place sheaves of wheat with berries at pew ends. For an informal affair, tie them off with strips of burlap. For a more formal celebration, braid gold ribbon around the stems or spray the wheat with gold paint.

- If you don't like the color of the church carpet, consider prelaying the aisle runner. Seat your guests from the side aisles and rope off the main aisle with a flower garland swagged on every other pew. Ushers can release the garland to let guests exit the main aisle after the ceremony.

- Use an assortment of angels in all shapes and sizes to adorn the pews as well as the altar.

- Arrange for candles placed in hurricane shades to preside over pew ends, making sure they won't obstruct anyone's view. Likewise, place hurricanes on window sills in boughs of evergreen.

- Place flat-backed hanging baskets at pew ends. Fill with dried flowers, fruits, and vegetables, leaving some to appear as if spilling from the basket.

- Add a Victorian touch to pews and candelabra with decorated antique lace fans.

- Cover the altar in a sea of poinsettias. Stack them in the shape of a Christmas tree for a holiday wedding.

- Keeping the season in mind, punctuate with pinecones in the winter and add blooming flowers in the spring.

- Flank the altar with urns on white columns. Fill with green arrangements. Or use columns to form an aisle for a home wedding.

- If you want a more intimate feel on your altar, fill in the space with ficus trees, blooming plants, and a variety of candelabra.

- State your love for one another under a archway of flowers.

Oh What to Wear

When selecting your wedding-day attire, it's best to choose timeless over trendy. Think about how your photos will look ten years from now. Although styles do change, there are many classic ways to express yourself.

- Consider a jacket and skirt combination for bridesmaids. Whether short or long, it at least has the potential of being worn again. Or choose a style that with a simple snip and a few stitches can transform into a lovely cocktail dress for future wearings. Fabrics such as crepe, lace, and silk can be elegant alternatives to prom-like taffeta.

- Put your bevy of bridesmaids into a rainbow of dress hues. Stick with the same basic color and have dresses graduate from light to dark.

- Pay close attention to back treatments on bridal attire. During many ceremonies, this is the view the congregation has for the longest amount of time.

- Provide the same material for each of your attendants if you would like an eclectic look for your bridesmaids. Leave the design of the dress up to each individual. Or simply request that each bridesmaid pick out a long, sleeveless dress in a given color scheme. Black and white is one simple color combination to consider.

- Suggest that the ever-growing flower girl wear a basic plain dress that she already owns. It can be transformed into wedding attire with a sash and a hair bow in wedding colors.

- Dress small ring bearers in shorts and knee socks. It's not only more comfortable, but protocol aficionados actually prefer it to a miniature tuxedo.

- Choose a color that makes a real statement. There's nothing that says a bride must wear white or ivory. A red or pale pink dress might be more your style.

- Select tear-away gowns which allow for more freedom and movement. These gowns appear to be long at first glance, but the over-skirt quickly snaps off to reveal a shorter skirt underneath.

- Make it a pristine affair with an all-white dress code for you and your guests.

- Add fur trim to your winter wedding dress. Your attendants and flower girl could also carry decorated fur muffs instead of bouquets.

- Embellish the tulle of the bridal veil with hand-painted flowers or another decorative design. Add real flowers to the train or headpiece.

- Embroider your name and wedding date into the slip you've borrowed from your mother. Add her name and date as well. Store afterwards for the next family bride and you've just started a new family tradition. The same would work on the ring bearer's pillow that has passed from one generation to another.

- Hire a seamstress to recreate your great-grandmother's wedding gown.

- Buy a vintage gown, but keep in mind the following: Before purchasing, make sure the gown is capable of withstanding any necessary alterations and dry cleaning. Seek the help of a professional if you have any doubts. Allow proper time for restoration and realize that a complete overhaul of the dress may prove impossible.

A Bunch of Flower Ideas

We've gathered some original concepts so you can pick your favorite.

- Explore designs from yesteryear including tussie-mussies and shower bouquets. Tussie-mussies are small nosegays housed in ornate keepsake holders while shower bouquets feature a waterfall of blossoms tied to ribbon streamers. A wedding ring bouquet, or wreath of flowers, is another option for the bride to carry, as is a bouquet-in-a-cloud where flowers are tucked into a cloud of netting.

- Incorporate out-of-the-ordinary items into your bridal bouquet design including cattails, seashells, and antique lace hankies.

- Use herbs and flowers for their given meanings. (See pages 71–72.)

- Utilize the bride's or bridesmaids' birthday flowers in bouquet design. (See flower-of-the-month chart on page 73.)

- Arrange artificial flowers in baskets. Each bridesmaid can take her arrangement home following the wedding.

- Start saving petals from all those flowers he sends you. Put the recycled petals to good use in the flower girl's basket. Or instead of throwing petals, the flower girl could hand individual flowers to the guests sitting at pew ends.

- Have several young attendants collectively carry a garland or rope of flowers.

- For a spring wedding, plan to have flower girls enter waving hoops decorated with flowers and ribbon. Likewise, use pomanders for a winter celebration.

- Have the ring bearer carry a calla lily in which the rings have been tied.

A Few Notes on Wedding Music

Here are some sharp ideas to make sure your celebration is far from flat.

- As a tribute to your parents, arrange to have a song from their weddings played during your wedding. Indicate this dedication in your program.

- Consider a string quartet to serve as a delightful prelude to your wedding ceremony. Likewise, a cellist, harpist, violinist, or flutist could serve the same purpose.

- If you're looking for something different when it comes to music, try a guitar solo or a vocal trio.

- Capture the attention of your guests with a trumpet or brass ensemble.

- Get your ceremony started on a beautiful note by employing the services of a young boys choir.

- Find a gospel choir to break into song as you're pronounced husband and wife.

- While your guests are waiting to be ushered out, entertain them with a bell choir. They're not only fascinating to listen to, they're also enjoyable to watch.

Creative Ceremony Concepts

To stand before friends and family and dedicate your life-long devotion to another person is to change your life forever. What special touches can be added to an already monumental occasion? Following is a list of just a few you may want to consider.

- Recruit a friend or hire someone to write a special song or poem for the two of you that can be performed or read on your wedding day.

- Stand out from the wedding crowd by picking a nonstandard start time for your festivities. Consider starting the ceremony at 7:10 P.M.—perhaps the exact time he proposed to you.

- Have attendants face out towards the congregation. The congregation will enjoy watching their faces and they, in turn, will enjoy being able to see yours.

- Request that your families stand and pledge their moral support for you as a couple. Likewise, if you're opposed to being "given away," your parents may instead promise their love and support to your new union.

- Arrange for a wreath of family and friendship to be placed at the altar. Request that each of your parents, siblings, and bridal party members lights a candle on the wreath. Explain in your program what the wreath means to you as a couple, emphasizing the importance of the continued love and support you will need from each of these important people in your new life together as husband and wife. These candles can be lit when family members or special friends walk into the room.

- Ask your mothers to light the single candles which accompany your unity candle during the prelude. Consider Greg Davis's "Parents' Prayer" as background music.

During the ceremony, you and the groom can use these individual candles to light your unity candle.

🐾 Write your own vows or perhaps a portion of them. Keep them short, sincere, and sweet. Share unique thoughts rather than trite metaphors. State what the union means to you personally and share what makes your love special as well as what you hope for the future. Consider ending with a confirmation of your commitment. If memorization isn't your strong card, have the vows scrolled onto a pretty piece of paper. Unroll yours at the appropriate moment for easy referral. In the end, you'll have a wonderful keepsake suitable for framing.

🐾 If you're both talented vocalists, sing your vows to one another, but keep in mind that nerves will already be at an all-time high. Your minister, priest, or rabbi could also chant part of the ceremony.

🐾 Invite your parents to renew their vows during your ceremony.

🐾 Stage a candlelight ceremony. To make this most effective, start your service at dusk or thereafter. Bridesmaids can carry bouquets featuring a candle in the middle. At a given time, the ushers or bride and groom can light the candles of those at pew ends. Each guest lights the candle of the person next to him until all candles are lit. This could be the perfect setting for wedding vows. When the officiant proclaims, "I now pronounce you husband and wife," candles can be blown out as lights come up.

🐾 Encourage children from previous marriages to play a special part in your wedding ritual. For instance, they could walk in with you during the processional, stand up with you, and even exchange rings or another special token. Consider presenting them with The Family Medallion, a pendant with three equally merged circles. To order medallions and an accompanying presentation ceremony entitled "Celebrating the New Family" call Clergy Services at (800) 237-1922.

🐾 Remember a loved one who has passed away with song, scripture, or prayer. If you would like to pay tribute to a deceased parent, a candle lit in his or her honor can further make the loved one's spirit a part of your special day. Include siblings in the lighting of this memory candle. A bouquet of flowers can also be displayed in a special place in memory of someone dear and a reference to the significance of the flowers can be placed in the program.

🐾 Host the ceremony on neutral ground in a marriage of mixed faiths. Explain various traditions and rituals to your mixed congregation in the program.

♣ Consider having your ceremony signed for hearing-impaired guests.

Making a Grand Entrance and Exit

This is the pomp and circumstance that royal weddings are made of. Let us offer some novel suggestions.

♣ Break tradition and greet your guests upon their arrival to the church.

♣ Jump the broomstick. If you're planning to incorporate this African tradition into your wedding festivities, invite your guests to help you decorate your broomstick with ribbons upon their arrival to your celebration. After all, according to superstition, ribbons tied in knots hold well wishes for the bride and groom. To order your very own decorated wedding broom, call Heritage Weddings at (800) 892-4297.

♣ Recruit a miniature bride and groom. Children serve in these roles, dressing exactly like their grownup counterparts.

♣ Prerecord a poem for your groom, perhaps one that speaks of your love for one another or being lifelong companions. Write your own or try excerpts from Robert Browning's *Rabbi Ben Ezra*. Play it on the church's sound system just before you walk down the aisle.

♣ For the home wedding, have bridesmaids serve as "human" columns, standing a few to each side holding garland to designate the aisle.

♣ Arrange for the groom to escort his mother in before the ceremony. As bride and groom, present roses to your parents as you exit the church. You may also leave a sentimental note for them in their respective pews.

♣ Have parents escort each other's spouses down the aisle as a part of the recessional to further emphasize a marriage of the two families.

♣ Arrange for the church bells to ring upon guests' arrival or departure from the church.

♣ Borrow from the English and race through an archway of anything from ski poles to boat oars as you leave the church. (See page 87 for more details.)

♣ Release a pair of love birds when you leave the church. Work with a reputable bird trainer. Inquire about different types of birds, keeping in mind both your needs and theirs. The birds may also remain in a pretty bird cage throughout the festivities. A butterfly release is another option; call Insect Lore at (800) 548-3284 for information.

- If your ceremony and reception sites are close in proximity, stage a musical procession of the entire bridal party and guests from one site to the other.

- Explore unique modes of transportation for your bridal party. Arrive at the reception in horse-drawn carriages or on a trolley. A motorcade of vintage cars or a fire truck could also get you to the church on time. A bride and groom who held their reception in an airplane hangar took that theme one step further by literally jetting off for their honeymoon in a small family plane. A helicopter could produce the same effect.

- If you don't want to keep your guests waiting, have the band leader instruct them to go through the buffet line upon their arrival at the reception. Thus, once you arrive, it's time to cut the cake and let the dancing begin. In other words, no down time.

- As an alternative to having the wedding party and parents announced by a master of ceremonies, make it more personal and memorable by handling the introductions yourselves. In between courses, you as a couple could introduce each attendant and tell a short story about how your friendship began. When introducing a sibling, perhaps share a childhood prank.

To Receive or Not to Receive?

That is the question. Here are some answers for the receiving line dilemma.

- A quick-paced solution to the traditional receiving line is to usher the guests out yourselves as bride and groom. Parents of the bridal pair may quickly receive at the back of the church. (A crowd of 425 was clocked out in less than thirty minutes this way from start to finish. Remember to keep the music playing.)

- If you don't do a receiving line, make sure you and your groom go to each table as a couple to thank your guests for coming.

- If you do a receiving line, give both sets of parents a list of those guests planning to attend your wedding. Write notations next to names explaining the guest's relationship to you or your family. It may help everyone with conversation in the receiving line, as well as later at the reception.

Beyond Caviar (Reception Menu Suggestions to Impress)

If you're hungry for something out of the ordinary, here's some food (and drink) for thought.

🐾 Offer a customized drink menu. Following are drink menu items as they were listed at a wedding where the stockbroker groom had proposed to the bride while scuba diving.

THE PLUNGE: A tribute to the bride and groom's underwater engagement, a special punch made just for you. (Little plastic fish came floating in this one.)

THE INFLATION HEDGER: The groom says take stock in Coca-Cola. Sprite, Diet Coke, and Coke available.

THE AGGRESSIVE INFLATION HEDGER: It's the above with a kick of rum or bourbon. (Drink stirrers with paper dollar bills attached like flags were found in this cocktail.)

Carry out the same idea at the buffet table. Put smaller versions of these menus at each guest's place setting.

🐾 Make your food the entertainment with fondue, lobsters, or a clambake. Eating with chopsticks might also provide an unusual twist.

🐾 In honor of your hunting hubby, serve up a wild-game buffet featuring an array of quail, pheasant, and duck dishes.

🐾 If you live in the Midwest, yet love traveling to the beach, consider offering the best of both worlds to your guests with a surf and turf menu, otherwise known as a sampling of seafood and beef.

🐾 Take your guests' palates on a tour around the country or world. Offer items such as Baltimore crabs and Kansas City strip steak, or Rome's fettuccine Alfredo and delicious French pastries. You could also offer a sampling of your city's finest with buffet tables from different restaurants.

🐾 Provide an omelet bar at your wedding breakfast.

🐾 Explore carved veggies and fruits for pretty and practical purposes. There are how-to books available for creating everything from cucumber sharks to watermelon luminaries. Items such as oranges, pumpkins, and squash can become unique serving dishes. Artichoke candle holders can also add a light touch.

- Cut breads and cheeses into special shapes such as wedding bells, doves, or hearts. Cookie cutters are one of the tricks of the trade.

- Serve uniquely-shaped pasta. Call The Pasta Shoppe at (800) 247-0188 to order their Love and Kisses pasta in heart and lip shapes.

- Bake muffins in heart-shaped tins.

- Add silk leaves to individual cake plates. Use lemon leaves, galax, or ruscus to decorate your buffet table. Mint leaves may add a refreshing touch to iced tea.

- Add strawberries or cherries to champagne for any toasts you might be planning. They are not only pretty, but taste good too. A champagne fountain might be another thought to entertain. Order extra champagne to toast future anniversaries together. Also provide a nonalcoholic spritzer so friends that don't drink may be equal participants during toasting rituals.

- Provide a coffee, tea, or cappuccino bar.

- Offer an extensive variety of imported beer and wine.

- Feature tapas dining where guests can sample spicy Spanish specialties. Have waiters deliver a variety of dishes to each table. A sampling of several can constitute a meal. Tapas dishes are known to be salty. Rumor has it they were originally made this way in the bars where they were served to get the patrons to drink more.

- Ask your caterer to create a food sculpture that can double as a decoration. Maybe it's a coral reef filled with tropical fish cut out of melons or hors d'oeuvres on sticks uniquely arranged on a head of lettuce to resemble an Indian head dress. Whatever you choose, it's sure to be a feast for the eye and palate.

- Artistically swirl chocolate onto dessert plates to add a delicious and decorative touch.

- Feature food stations where a wide variety of foods are available. Remember these stations can tie to any wedding theme. For instance, you could take your guests on an edible journey through European countries or island hopping in the Pacific Ocean.

- Serve the same meal that you enjoyed on your first date together and let your guests in on the secret.

- Provide special diet menu items for guests who are watching their cholesterol and fat intake.

☙ Make sure your florist and caterer work hand in hand so that everything will coordinate. (Fresh flowers can take a swim in your punch bowl in a heart-shaped ice ring or on a smaller scale, in ice cubes. Or flowers can be found resting on cake layers.)

☙ Press flowers between two clear glass serving plates.

☙ Use grape clusters and loaves of French bread to fill in gaps on your buffet table.

☙ Incorporate edible flower petals into desserts and other entrees. Edible varieties include roses, nasturtiums, Johnny-jump-ups (pansies), violets, carnations, marigolds, chrysanthemums, and snapdragons. Sugar coat or paint the petals with chocolate for an extra sweet effect. Be sure to wash the flowers, using those which are free from dirt and pesticides.

☙ Keep uninvited guests away from your outdoor wedding with nature's bug repellents including mint, marigolds, geraniums, and rue. Citronella candles are also available in all shapes and sizes.

*I*deas to Take the Cake

Some couples show their creativity with cake by the way they smear the first piece onto their mate's face. However, there are many other ways you can express yourself. Following are some ideas for you to nibble on.

☙ Wedding cakes are not always white. They can even be mousse or perhaps a different flavor on each tier. They can also reflect a common interest of the bride and groom. The scuba-diving couple had a groom's cake shaped like a shark. The main cake had blue icing and featured other edible iced sculptures in an ocean motif. For the man that likes to play the links, a groom's cake that looks like a sloping green would draw cheers from the gallery.

☙ The porcelain miniature bride and groom that topped your mother and father's cake many years ago could be placed on top of yours today. Or you may choose a topper which represents the way the two of you met. For example, if a charity run first brought the two of you together, then a small pair of running shoes could be the answer. If you were high school or college sweethearts, mini pompoms and a pennant in your school colors could do the trick. One groom had presented the bride's engagement ring in a seashell as they were walking along the beach. In turn, that same treasured shell found its way to the top tier of their wedding cake. A precious Waterford, Lladró or other collectible, such as the angel that topped your first birthday cake, can also serve as extraordinary cake toppers. The baseball or hockey fan may also appreciate a personalized piece of sports memorabilia. Watch your local paper for celebrity signings or charity appearances for your chance to obtain an autograph. Or write to your favorite celebrities.

❧ Send your guests home with a piece of cake. Place a personalized label on the box or tissue paper that holds the cake. Or design your own unique boxes using sponge paint or decoupage. Print your names and wedding date or a favorite quotation on the label. According to tradition, the unmarried who sleep with this under their pillow will dream of the person they will marry. Cake can also be sent to guests unable to attend the wedding.

Favorite Favors and Other Special Keepsakes

Weddings are all about memories—both old and new. To help you and your guests remember this cherished day for years to come, consider utilizing one or more of the following ideas.

❧ Give each guest a candle. Attach a note requesting they light it sometime and say a prayer for you and the groom.

❧ Make personalized chocolate kiss favors. First place a chocolate kiss in netting, then replace the white strip of paper with a similar piece of paper that features the bridal couple's names and wedding date. Tie up with narrow ribbon.

❧ Send guests home with a tree seedling to plant in honor of your wedding. They will be reminded of your love for years to come. (To order, see page 13.)

❧ Arrange for guests to say farewell with a 21-bubble salute as you leave the reception. Decorative labels featuring the bride and groom's names and wedding date can be placed around child-size bubble bottles and given to guests upon their arrival at the reception.

❧ Pay homage to your ethnic heritage. The Irish bride can say thank you to her guests by giving each a blooming shamrock plant upon their departure. (Ethnic traditions begin on page 81.)

❧ Present a special herb to the groom's guests and another to the bride's. Select herbs with sweet meanings. Attach the name of the herb and its symbolism on a gift tag. (Herbs were an important part of weddings past. For the meanings assigned to various herbs, see pages 71–72.)

- Send guests home with one of Grandma's famous cinnamon rolls, and attach her secret recipe.

  (Other favor suggestions can be found throughout the theme wedding section beginning on page 4 and later in the do-it-yourself section starting on page 51.)

- Have guests sign a tablecloth at the reception. Year after year you will be able to put your tablecloth of memories to good use at anniversary dinners. Embroider over signatures to make sure they won't fade. Along the same lines, have guests sign a photo mat you can use later to frame one of your favorite wedding pictures.

- Circulate a journal at your reception and ask guests to write a little something to the bride and groom. The end result will be a wonderful keepsake, something like your high school yearbook.

- Looking for an alternative to throwing the bouquet and garter? Consider presenting them to some important people. Attach a gold heart charm on which their name has been engraved. Or throw several smaller bouquets, perhaps one for each of your bridesmaids. (This tradition was quite popular in nineteenth-century America. Incorporate the charms as suggested for use in the charm cake on pages 41–42.)

Tripping the Light Fantastic and Other Entertaining Activities

Whether you hire a ragtime pianist or a barbershop quartet, you are sure to leave your guests' toes tapping. Following are some other ideas to entertain.

- Hire a pianist or strolling musicians to add life to your cocktail or dinner hour without adding a sour note to your budget. For a whimsical touch, consider a player piano, jukebox, or accordion.

- Explore all the band possibilities which include Motown, Jazz, Rhythm and Blues, Reggae, Big Band, Dixieland, Country, and Top 40. Hire more than one band and have them split the evening. Throw in a dance instructor and you'll really keep your guests involved. Keep the band leader posted on the evening's activities to help him better serve as your emcee.

- Honor parents by having the band play the first-dance songs from their weddings or dedicate the "Anniversary Waltz" to them.

- Do a variation on the traditional dollar dance. You may forgo the money, but still invite people to line up for short dances with the bride and groom. (During the traditional dollar dance, guests pay to dance with the bride or groom. Money raised is for the honeymoon.)

- Learn a unique dance step as bride and groom and wow your friends and family during the first dance. Better yet, make it a family affair and have your parents join you at the lessons to help them become better acquainted.

- Keep the party swinging while the guests await the arrival of the bridal party with a comedian, song-leader, or square dance caller. Karaoke is another popular way to pass the time.

- Let the dancing begin if the receiving line will take awhile. You can always break for the traditional first dance of the bride and groom later.

- Ask your guests to participate in a caption contest. While entertaining, it can also provide a picturesque overview of the bride and groom's lives. To hold a caption contest, simply display a montage of photos of the bride and groom taken throughout the years. To maximize participation, assign a given photo to a group of guests and instruct them to write a caption by that photo. Judges will pick the top three captions and prizes will be awarded.

- Captivate your guests with a childhood video or slide show at the reception or rehearsal. For the groom that has everything, this could be the perfect surprise from the bride. Do it yourself or enlist the help of a video production company. To add an unusual twist, consider using a newscast format for the video. To carry out this theme, have a family member or close friend act as a reporter to narrate the events. Remember, the funnier the pictures, the more your guests will enjoy the video. Top the present off with a storage case decorated with your engagement newspaper clippings and favorite pictures. (One bride's uncle, a photographer, made a childhood slide show of the bride and groom. By the time the show made its debut at the reception, he had added a final slide showing the bride and groom walking down the aisle. Talk about goose bumps!)

- For background music to a wedding video or slide show consider rock-and-roll favorites such as Paul Anka's "Let The Bells Keep Ringing," The Beach Boys' "Wouldn't It Be Nice," Don Cherry's "Band Of Gold," Buddy Clark's "I'll Dance At Your Wedding," and "When We Get Married" by The Dreamlovers.

🐾 Catch your groom by surprise by recruiting your creative bridesmaids to perform a song or skit dedicated to him.

🐾 Play a popular wedding game. Encourage each table of guests to think of songs with the word "love" in them. Throughout the evening, they can stand and sing the song. The bride and groom are expected to kiss when they get to the word "love."

🐾 Have a family friend emcee the important details of your special day.

$\mathcal{P}$laces Everyone

There are a variety of ways to seat your guests. Your reception will get started on the right foot if you've taken the time to think through this important detail. While musical chairs may be one option, here are some more practical suggestions.

🐾 Scale down the head table to an intimate table for two — the bride and groom. The best part about this setup is that your attendants will get to be seated with their dates.

🐾 Use favorite childhood pictures of the bride and groom on place cards. Have the groom's picture printed in one half of a heart on some of the place cards and the bride's picture in the other half of the heart on the rest of the place cards. When two guests' place cards are put together, the heart will become whole (see illustration).

Table No. 14

🐾 Assign guests to note a funny story about the bride or groom on the place card. At an appropriate time, have them share the information on their card with the others at their table. The sharing makes for a wonderful ice-breaker.

🐾 Seat guests at tables named after famous love and wedding songs. Instruct the band to play these songs throughout the evening. When each plays, that table should be asked to dance. Draw the seating chart in the shape of a musical note and arrange the tables to correspond.

🐾 If children will be invited to your reception, designate a special table for them where kid-oriented dishes such as hot dogs and ice cream are served.

(Additional seating suggestions can be found throughout the theme wedding section beginning on page 4.)

Delightful Decorations for Your Reception

Whether you plan to do the decorating yourself or hire outside help, the following ideas can get you started.

- Create a carousel effect at your reception. Set tables in circle formation and decorate a carousel horse to sit at each table's center. Put a tall pole in the center of the room and have ribbons streaming from the pole to each table's centerpiece. On a smaller scale, the carousel centerpiece could have ribbons streaming to each individual's place card.

- If the climate and lead time are right, grow flowers and plants at home to use in your decorations. For instance, if you are planning a spring garden wedding at home in the Midwest, fill your garden with tulip bulbs in your wedding colors during the fall prior to your wedding. Evergreen can be cut and utilized in winter decorations.

- Use cabanas to provide shade at an outdoor wedding.

- Attach greenery with white tulle to chair backs and columns.

- Drape yards of tulle from the ceiling or skywalks to create an overhead oasis of heavenly clouds.

- Weave tulle and strands of pearls around votive candles for table centerpieces. (Remember to keep material away from flame.)

- Create tulle overskirts for tables by first covering each table with a tablecloth in wedding colors. Sprinkle with fresh flower petals before adding tulle overlay. Swag tulle overlay with flower clusters.

- String ribbon and cowrie shells through the edges of lace tablecloths. Within some African cultures, these shells are thought to bring good luck. (For more African wedding traditions, turn to page 81.)

- Set your dance floor apart with a trellis, archway, or gazebo covered in viny smilax or fresh flowers.

- For the country setting, use a collection of quilts for tablecloths. For the Victorian wedding, use a collection of lace tablecloths.

- For an Oriental feel, add Japanese paper lanterns to light strands (see illustration). You can take this theme one step further by using bonsai trees as table centerpieces.

- Consider tear-away centerpieces, perhaps a basket filled with small potted plants or flowers which your guests can take home as keepsakes.

- Fill crystal bowls, compotes, or vases with colorful glass ornaments. Place the ornaments on a bed of metallic streamers. To complete the illusion, flank the arrangement with candlesticks.

- Float candles and flowers in decorative bowls of water placed on table mirrors.

- Form an interesting tablescape by using a variety of colors, shapes, and sizes of candle groupings.

- Light the way for your guests with tiki torches or luminaries. Use carved pumpkins if you're getting married close to Halloween.

- Explore different lighting options such as up lights, down lights, spotlights, and color gels. You can even experiment with battery-operated closet lights and clamp-on bedside lights. You can also achieve a nice effect by simply replacing an ordinary bulb with a color bulb. Determine key focal points. Remember that not enough light can be hazardous, while too much light can make a room seem uninviting.

- Incorporate floating lily pads into poolside celebrations.

- Wire blooming flowers to a bush that hasn't quite reached its peak or to one that doesn't ordinarily bloom.

- Put topiaries on table tops, at entry ways, or use several to outline your dance floor. They come in all shapes, sizes, and colors. Those made into hearts or wedding bells may be especially appropriate. (See page 54 for simple instructions on how to make a topiary.)

- Mix opposites for a dramatic effect. Put a small tree branch in a vase and add ornate roses. The combination will make for beautiful centerpieces.

- Since variety is the spice of life, consider putting table arrangements in a collection of vases, baskets, teapots, pitchers, or copper pots. Use a variety of shapes and sizes at each table. Each arrangement will make a statement all its own.

- Place a goldfish bowl at every table for a unique centerpiece and conversation piece.

- Fill small trees with ornaments for the people sitting at each table. Place in the center of each table and instruct guests to select a favor from the tree at the end of the evening. (Remember that you're not limited to just Christmas with this idea.)

- Enchant guests with strands of little white lights. Add them against black material to the band's backdrop, place them on ficus trees lining the dance floor, or string them along the ceiling to create a starry-night effect.

- Customize each table centerpiece, keeping in mind the commonalties of the guests who will be seated at that table. For example, if the college sorority sisters will be seated together, have the table decorated in the sorority's colors and flowers. If your fellow nursing friends will be dining together, then an all-white table with bandages and get-well cards scattered about would be appropriate.

- Top tables with collections of clowns, dolls, masks, globes, garden urns, candlesticks, Santas, cacti, or antique sports memorabilia.

- Fill wheel barrows and carts with potted flowers and place throughout reception facility.

- Cater your table decorations to the bride and groom. Each table could depict a different memory from the bride and groom's past. For example, at one table the bride's pompoms might team with a photo of her in a cheerleading outfit. The groom's equivalent might be his Little League glove and team picture.

- Bring elegance to your buffet table with an ice sculpture. The couple who used their baby photos on their wedding invitations also had their childhood signatures carved into a heart-shaped ice sculpture (see illustration). An ice sculpture shaped as a vase can also be lovely, especially when it holds the same flowers used in the bride's bouquet.

- Add different levels to the buffet table by stashing boxes and crates under material overlays. Or instead of hiding the crates, you can decorate them by painting, stenciling, or wallpapering in your wedding colors.

- Host a contest to give away the table centerpieces. Perhaps the person with a sticker on the inside of his place card wins. Or host a different contest for each table from dance competitions to trivia about the bride and groom. Another option is to have leftover centerpieces taken to a local nursing home.

- At a private facility, add fresh bouquets of flowers to the restrooms for an unexpected touch. Pretty soaps, monogrammed towels, and candles will also leave the ladies' room aglow.

$\mathcal{S}$ay Cheese
(A Focus on Original Photo and Video Concepts)

Your photographs and video will help you tell the story of your wedding day forever. We've put together some ideas to help you capture these once-in-a-lifetime moments.

- Look through your mother and father's wedding photos. Is there a tradition you would like to continue? Maybe there's a beautiful picture of your grandmother fixing your mother's veil on her wedding day. Stage the same by having your mother or grandmother fix yours for the camera. Have it developed in black and white to make the resemblance even more apparent. (See how easily traditions can begin.)

- Schedule all of your pictures to be taken before the ceremony for an earlier start to the reception. However, if you don't want the groom to see you before you walk down the aisle (in some circles, it is considered bad luck), consider arranging some private time together before the pictures begin. At a designated time, clear the rest of the bridal party away and have him stand at the altar. You can then make your way down the aisle. In effect, he gets a private showing. If everyone respects your privacy, this can prove to be the most special time you spend together as a couple on your wedding day. If appropriate, talk with your minister to see if communion for just the two of you can be arranged.

- Pose for an all-time favorite wedding photo which features the bride and groom kissing. Young attendants are covering their mouths with their hands as if they've caught the bridal pair doing something they shouldn't be doing.

- Explore hot trends in photography such as hand-colored portraits and those shot in sepia tones. The end result is a timeless treasure.

- Write a short poem on a heart gift tag and tie to disposable cameras placed on reception tables. Some of the best pictures are the unplanned ones. Example poem:

While <u>Betty</u> and <u>Bob</u> dance,
Don't leave photos just to chance.
Shoot many pictures for good measure,
The bride and groom want lots to treasure.

♣ If you had your dress made, have a photo album covered in the same fabric as a resting place for the candids you will accumulate. One mother who made her daughter's wedding gown also made a photo album and pearled it the same way she did the dress.

♣ Make sure someone snaps photos of you when you're trying on dresses for the scrapbook. The same goes if you're having the dress made. You'll treasure looking back on your dress in its various stages.

♣ If your parents' and grandparents' marriages have stood the test of time, consider paying tribute to them by displaying their wedding photos.

♣ Recruit friends to shoot candids during the rehearsal dinner and wedding-day festivities. Keep cameras clicking in the bride and groom's dressing rooms before the wedding too.

♣ Enlist a friend to take Polaroid pictures of each guest with the bride and groom as well as group pictures of each table. Design a funny sandwich board into which attending couples can stick their heads and pose for a photo (see illustration).

Go'n to the Chapel

♣ Print keepsake photo folders in honor of your special occasion. Hire a photographer to take pictures of guests upon their arrival to the reception. Have them developed and ready for pick up toward the end of the reception.

♣ Save memorabilia from each stage of your wedding, from fabric swatches to boarding passes, and use in your scrapbook in addition to your photographs.

♣ Hook up a video camera to a big screen television and catch your guests by surprise throughout the evening. The finished tape will also be a great keepsake. Plan to show video highlights of your wedding festivities at an anniversary celebration.

♣ Arrange for someone to shoot video at each table to gather commentary from all of your family and friends. Set up one stationary camera for this purpose and throughout the evening remind guests to pay a visit.

The Icing on the Cake

Now that you've covered the basics in formulating your wedding strategy, here are a few extras for your consideration. In this section we'll offer thoughtful gift ideas in addition to clever thematic notions for your bridesmaids' luncheon and rehearsal dinner. And finally, we'll teach you how to make delightful decorations and fantastic favors.

Sweet Surprises

Sometimes it's the simple things that mean so much. Never is this more true than when it comes to weddings. Try any one of the following random acts of sweetness.

- Make baby-sitting arrangements for your out-of-town guests traveling with small children, for both rehearsal and wedding-day activities. If you're planning a hotel reception, see if you can have an extra room incorporated into your package for this purpose. Arrange for entertainment and pizza.

- If it's available, make arrangements for guests to stay at a bed and breakfast in your area. It might make them feel more at home, while providing a vacation atmosphere.

- Surprise your attendants with snacks on the big day. Everything will go a lot smoother if tummies aren't rumbling. Keep it simple unless you plan to provide full-body bibs.

- Hire a hairdresser for the day to do up-do's for your bridesmaids.

- As a couple, keep focused. Remember why you are getting married and take time out for special dates where wedding talk is not allowed. Consider a night at home alone and don't forget to unplug the phone as you enjoy your candlelight dinner. Or instead, plan a night on the town for two with all the trimmings. (Don't forget the limo. Tell your groom you need to practice getting in and out of one before the big day arrives.)

Charming Ideas for Your Bridesmaids' Luncheon

This is the time for you and your friends to share memories and create new ones. Invite nostalgia with any of the following ideas.

- Borrow from the past to serve up fun with a special charm cake. Buy a silver charm for each bridesmaid and any other special guests that may be attending. Insert charms into the cake and then ice. Some traditional charms and their supposed fortunes include: a ring (next to marry), coin (good fortune), heart (romance), wishbone (your wish will come true), and a button (old maid). Charm sets are available through the Exclusively Weddings Catalog at (800) 759-7666, Dept. BK. Let creativity be your guide and you can make changes or additions to this tradition. Start shopping for charms and the symbolism will fall into place. Of course, you can always personalize the charms to the individual participants. Warn guests to nibble gently. Ribbons may also be attached to the charms before they are inserted in the cake. Each guest can gently pull on the ribbon to remove the charm.

- Have a tea party just like you did when you were a little girl. Have everyone play dress-up to really make the event authentic. Send the invitations with a toy tea cup complete with a real tea bag. For favors, select a unique teapot for each or fill an antique cup and saucer with an orchid bloom. (An old tradition calls for a teacup to be given as an engagement present from a fiancé to his beloved. When they are apart she is to drink from the cup, if ever it should overflow or break, then she knows he has been unfaithful. Attach a card explaining this tradition.)

- Take your tea party in a different direction with a Mad Hatter theme. Encourage everyone to wear an outrageous hat, and award a prize for the most creative millinery treasure. Play *Alice in Wonderland* quietly in the background. Serve the Queen of Heart's tarts and put "drink me" on beverage glasses. For invitations, write "Don't be late for a very important date!" as the headline on a cut-out rabbit invitation attached to a toy watch.

- Have a potato or dessert bar party.

- Schedule a bridesmaids' slumber party. Ask guests to bring old photographs, 45's, and cassettes to ensure lots of reminiscing. A Victorian bed and breakfast could be the perfect setting for nostalgia to unfold.

- Utilize a picture of the bride as a flower girl on the front of the bridesmaids' luncheon invitation. Or find a yesteryear picture of the bride in hair rollers for the front of a card inviting the bridesmaids to a day of beauty. Send a bottle of nail polish with the invitation. While the frugal budget may call for you to paint each other's nails, the more elaborate budget might include a trip to a spa.

- Host a tasting party for all of your attendants in lieu of individual bachelor and bachelorette parties. In this arrangement, friends of the opposite sex may also be better accommodated. Sample champagne, wine, appetizers, and cake that you are considering for your reception. Let them help you make the final selection.

One-of-a-Kind Rehearsals

Since your wedding seems nothing short of a Broadway production at times, you'll want to make sure you receive rave reviews from your fans by hosting a memorable cast party. In fact, while we're on the subject of plays, did you know that the bride, for superstitious reasons, used to call in an understudy to play her part at the rehearsal? You could follow suit, but we're sure you'll want to participate in any one of the following rehearsal themes which can easily translate into fun at your engagement party as well.

🐝 Consider making your rehearsal dinner a casual event if your wedding-day plans are formal. Your bridal party will be especially thankful. Have theme T-shirts printed for your bridal party to wear. For favors, have plastic cups printed with the bride and groom's names, wedding date, and caricatures.

🐝 If most of your bridal party will not be in town until the day of the wedding, host a rehearsal breakfast the day of instead of a dinner the night before.

🐝 Stage a barbecue or picnic for your rehearsal dinner. Both can be held indoors and would be a nice break from a cold winter. All it takes is a little imagination. In the case of a picnic, send plastic ants with a red and white checkered invitation, or write invitation details on a note card attached to a piece of green artificial turf. Borrow picnic baskets and quilts from friends and fill with surprises.

🐝 For your black and white wedding, consider a "Most Wanted" theme for your rehearsal dinner. Design a "Most Wanted" poster featuring the mugs of your bridal party and family members. Give each a funny nickname such as "Donna the I-Do" for the bride and "I'm-Headed-for-the-Poor-House Bob" for the bride's father. Everyone should be assigned a convict number which can be incorporated into place cards and name tags. Black and white striped tablecloths can top off your theme. (Don't be surprised if your groom shows up in a ball and chain.)

🐝 If your first date was to a carnival, recreate that atmosphere at your rehearsal. Obvious additions to your buffet table should be cotton candy and caramel apples. An ice-cream buffet where hot fudge sundaes and banana splits can be made-to-order would also be a welcome treat. Send invitations in popcorn boxes. Simple carnival games such as "tossing the rings over the bottle tops," "picking up the floating numbered duck," or "throwing darts at balloons" could mean small prizes for your guests. Recruit a friend to oversee the playing of these throughout the evening so you're not left with the juggling act. Speaking of which, juggling clowns and a face-painter would provide ready entertainment for children. Mimes would also leave your guests talking.

🍀 If your wedding will occur during the height of football season, add football stickers to the place cards, inflatable footballs to the ceiling, and serve Gatorade to the guests. (Be careful—a really fun party might end in a Gatorade shower for the groom.) Following is an invitation that was used with this theme.

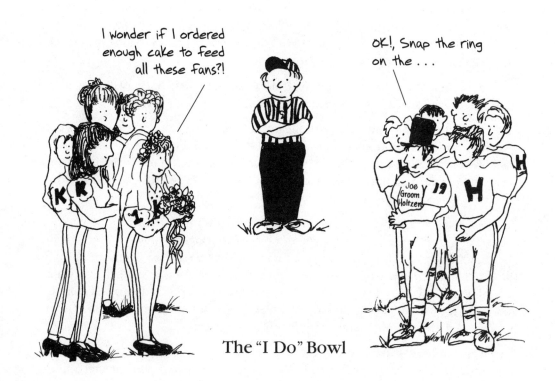

The "I Do" Bowl

🐾 Offer a sampling of food emblematic of where you live, especially if many of your guests are from out-of-town. In Kansas City, barbecue would be a must. The same holds true for Cajun in Louisiana and pizza in Chicago. Invite your guests to "get a taste of your city" by gluing your invitation to a map of the city. Roll the map and secure by tying a plastic fork to it with a ribbon. If you live in a place that's exciting to visit, you can take this theme a step further by inviting your guests to come in a day early for a bus tour of the city. The bride and groom can emcee the action-packed afternoon while catching up with guests before the wedding-day craziness begins. Give snow globes of a special landmark as favors.

🐾 Follow your rehearsal with a hay ride and bonfire. Set the stage by inserting strands of hay into the invitation envelopes. Roast marshmallows and hot dogs. Hire a square-dance caller and really swing your partners. Cowboy boots and jeans are a must.

🐾 Design your rehearsal invitation as a spinoff on a children's school play. The invitation's front could feature a drawing which depicts a scene from a typical children's play. The invitation copy could call the participants together for a dress rehearsal. (Opening night is wedding day.) The invite could be written in little kids' handwriting and decorated with crayon drawings.

🐾 Help guests find good fortune by serving Chinese cuisine at your rehearsal dinner, complete with personalized fortune cookies that send best wishes to the new bride and groom and thanks to those attending. Keeping with this theme, tie chopsticks with red ribbon to a rolled invitation which also reads like a fortune cookie.

🐾 Transport your guests to a deserted island by hosting your rehearsal dinner poolside at the hotel where your guests are staying. Send your rolled invitations in empty bottles requesting that guests join you on Honeymoon Isle. Place blue cloths on the tables, add cutout fish, then cover with a fish net and adorn with seashells. Offer Caribbean cuisine, while guests drink from coconuts and listen to the sounds of Jimmy Buffet or a steel drum band.

🐾 Make a splash with a pool party even where there is no pool. Send your invitations attached to a pair of water wings or a child's floatie ring. Fill kiddie pools with ice to serve as beer coolers. Bottles of suntan lotion and sunscreen can serve as place cards. Tie nose plugs around napkins.

🐾 Host a Hawaiian luau in honor of the pending nuptials. Send the invite on a vacation postcard or brochure from Hawaii. Adorn your bridal party members and their guests with flower leis. Serve fresh pineapple slices in glasses of iced tea. Use grass skirts to hide unsightly coolers and trash cans. With the best man's help, a hula dance by the groomsmen in grass skirts would make for a festive party.

- ♣ Plan a sock hop. Send invitations die-cut in the shape of an old 45 record asking guests to dress in fifties attire. Serve up root beer floats.

- ♣ Make it a family affair and include the kids. During the actual rehearsal you can have a puppet show staged in the church basement to keep them entertained, or have the kids create a puppet show that they can perform later that evening for the adults. If you choose the latter, you will need to provide the puppets or the materials to make them.

- ♣ Host a New Orleans-style jazz funeral to symbolically lay to rest your single days. A jazz funeral was one way poor folks in the South were buried when they didn't have any family. Donations were made at the local pub for a deceased friend's funeral. Next, a procession complete with jazz musicians would take the deceased to his final resting place. This type of celebration was always viewed as a happy rather than a sad occasion. At your jazz funeral, feature old-time gospel songs such as "Down by the Riverside" and "When the Saints Go Marching In." Hire a professional mourner to dress the part and weep throughout the evening's activities. Add spice to your evening by serving a combination of Creole, crawfish, and gumbo. Use Mardi Gras masks as place cards and give beads as favors.

Special Gifts for Special People

How do you begin to say thank you to the people who have played an important role in your life as well as your wedding? You can begin by sending them thank-you postcards from your honeymoon. Following are other ways you can show your appreciation. (To add a special bow to gift items, turn to page 53.)

Gifts for Mom and Dad

- ♣ Remember Mom and Dad with a special gift. In making her daughter's bridal gown, one bride's mother had sewn on nearly 28,000 pearls by hand. The bride recognized this special labor of love by giving her a mother's ring. Appropriately, the ring featured a pearl, which was also the bride's birthstone. Mom might also enjoy a makeover, manicure, or massage.

❧ Arrange to have thank-you bouquets sent to parents the day after your wedding.

❧ Give a music box that plays a song from your wedding with an engraved message.

Gifts for the Bridal Party

❧ Show your friends how important their participation in your wedding is to you. Consider asking your best friend to be your maid of honor with a poem you've written or found as a tribute to your friendship. Or write the poem in a photo album. Include a collection of photos that traces your friendship through the years. Obviously, wedding photos will be added later.

❧ Shortly before the wedding, present personalized handkerchiefs to each of your bridesmaids. You'll probably get a laugh, but odds are they'll also be put to good use. Include the mothers in this exchange. Monogrammed stationery and birthstone jewelry are other options. (See the birthstone chart on page 67.)

❧ Provide panty hose for the big day in addition to the common gift of earrings for the bridesmaids. In each girl's present also include something unique to her or your friendship. Perhaps give her a copy of the classic movie that always makes both of you cry.

❧ Personalize the way you wrap each attendant's present. For the traveler, wrap her gift in a map. The stock broker groomsman will be surprised to find his present tucked away in the *Wall Street Journal,* and the bridesmaid who loves to laugh will be tickled pink to find hers amongst the comics.

❧ Pay a visit to your local antique store or flea market to select a piece of antique silverware for each bridesmaid. If she's already married and the piece happens to feature her new last initial, she'll treasure it all the more. For your single bridesmaids, it's a wonderful addition to their trousseaus.

❧ Present the bridesmaids with matching monogrammed robes to be worn in the bride's room while getting ready for the ceremony.

❧ Give each bridesmaid a beautiful vase. Send her a bouquet of flowers immediately following your wedding and then again on her birthday.

❧ Place gift baskets in attendants' hotel rooms. Fill the baskets with goodies symbolic of the city where the wedding is taking place. Baskets filled with some basics such as bottled water and snacks would be appreciated by out-of-town attendants staying in the homes of friends and relatives. For those planning an extended stay, include a city map, a list of events, and coupons for local eats and treats. Enclose a flyer you've designed of interesting landmarks and entertainment options. Include a pineapple which stands for hospitality.

- If all of your attendants celebrate Christmas, present each with a stocking, regardless of the time of year your wedding occurs. (According to legend, the birth of the Christmas stocking has its own ties to marriage. Saint Nicholas presented the very first Christmas stockings to a poor man's daughters because they had no dowries. He filled each with gold coins. Although gold coins may put you a little over budget, you can fill yours with other treasures.) The stockings can also be personalized and homemade if you're really ambitious. Attach a note which tells about the origin of the stocking.

- In addition, recruit someone to gather leftovers at the end of the reception to put in small take-home baskets for your out-of-town bridal party members. It will be a lot less expensive for them to snack from that versus the minifridge in their hotel room. They'll appreciate your thoughtfulness.

- Give bridal party members lottery tickets with a note expressing how lucky you are to have their friendship.

- Incorporate birthday flowers into gift items. Embroider each bridesmaid's birthday flower onto a keepsake for her. Likewise, give bulbs or a flowering plant to each attendant so she can enjoy her birthday flowers beyond your wedding day. Or top each bridesmaid's present with an artificial stem of her birthday flower. (See the chart of birthday flowers on page 73.)

- Engrave or personalize your bridal party gifts so for years to come your attendants will remember who gave them the gift. (They may even remember to send you an anniversary card.)

- Relate gifts to wedding themes. If, for instance, you and your groom are staging a Christmas wedding, consider giving each of your attendants a unique Christmas ornament. Dated collectibles are always treasured. Stay cognizant of the different religious backgrounds of your attendants. For the wine theme wedding, wine racks would be appropriate. In conjunction with a period wedding, you could present a hand-painted parasol to each bridesmaid or arrange to have an antique piece of jewelry incorporated into each bridesmaid's bouquet. And for the sporty wedding, tickets to the ball park would be a hit.

❧ If you and your bridesmaids have been dieting for the big day, make post-wedding plans to celebrate your chiseled waistlines at an all-you-can-eat pizza buffet or give each girl a piece of individually wrapped chocolate as a reward.

❧ Utilize the Japanese art of *furoshiki* by making the wrapping of your present a gift in itself. Instead of using paper gift wrap, the Japanese swaddle presents in beautiful silk scarves tied in special knots.

Gifts for Special Friends and Family

❧ Present a corsage or boutonniere to friends or family members who may not be a part of the bridal party, but who have gone the extra mile to make your wedding special. Your godparents might also appreciate the sentiment.

❧ Prepare gift baskets as your way of saying thanks to the people who have played an important part in your wedding-day festivities. Consider their interests, hobbies, favorite foods, and go from there. Following are some fun-filled basket ideas.

> **"Nuts About You"** - Fill with spiced almonds, vanilla-nut flavored coffee, a recipe for pecan pie, a book about nuts, and a Christmas nutcracker.

> **"Keep in Touch"** - Fill with note cards, an address book, a special occasion reminder book, stamps, and a pretty pen.

> **"A Day in the Park"** - Fill a picnic basket with wine, cheese, a pretty tablecloth, and a Frisbee.

The same can be done for your friend the seamstress, artist, or chef. Keep in mind you don't always have to use a basket. For a friend that loves movies, you could fill a personalized popcorn bowl with some microwave popcorn, movie tickets, videos, and a subscription to *People*. For a friend with a green thumb, personalize a watering can and fill with decorated gardening gloves, a small shovel, and packets of seeds. Hat boxes, which come in a variety of sizes, can also be the perfect containers.

❧ Bring or send a small gift to each hostess of every shower that is given for you. An appropriate and clever hostess gift might be an umbrella. Attach a note to thank her for giving you a "shower."

❧ For the shut-in relative who could not attend the festivities, send a pressed flower from a centerpiece or your bouquet with a note reminding them they were missed, but not far from your thoughts. A picture placed in a special frame might help them feel like they were there as well.

- For the friend who has really worked her fingers to the bone, put together a bag of goodies she can use to pamper herself. Include items such as lotion, nail files, bubble bath, bath pillow, candles, easy-listening music, chocolates, and champagne. Or make arrangements for a day of beauty at a local salon.

- Give a gift that keeps on giving every month of the year by enrolling your special someone in Coffee Quest, a gourmet coffee-of-the-month club. Call (800) 205-JAVA for more information.

Gifts for the Groom

- Have a quilt made for the groom from a collection of childhood memories including sports ribbons, camp T-shirts, and Little League uniforms.

- Present your groom with a time capsule of what was in the news at the time of your wedding. Seal it and make plans to open it on your silver wedding anniversary.

- Decorate a shaker or hat box for you and your groom to house your wedding memories. Stencil your names and wedding date on the front. Add hearts and flowers. Select a larger box to hold everything from the guest book to the souvenirs you collect on your honeymoon. A recycled popcorn tin works great too.

- Surprise your groom with cards, notes, poems, or small presents throughout the wedding planning months. Or show up at the office and steal him away for a surprise picnic lunch. This will show him that although the wedding ceremony is important, he is most important. Don't forget to put a special note under his pillow the night before the wedding. With the note, leave a bottle of wine to be opened on your first anniversary. Or fill his bedroom or entire apartment with red balloons. Attach or insert a love note to each one. (Many party supply stores now carry disposable helium tanks that are inexpensive and easy to transport.)

- Prepare a scrapbook of your courtship. Or decoupage a keepsake box with tickets from movies, plays, or sporting events you've attended together. Fill the box with love notes.

A Gift Idea for You

- Treat yourself and have the lucky penny or sixpence from your shoe turned into a pendant for a necklace or a charm for your bracelet. A company called 12/31 berez can also turn champagne caps, commemorating your wedding toast, into custom-designed jewelry including necklaces, earrings, or a set of cuff links. Call (310) 394-3922 for prices and ordering information.

ⅅo-It-Yourself
(Make Anything from Simple Gifts to Decorations)

You may have noted that you can make many of the things already listed in this book. In addition you may want to try your hand at creating some of the following beginner-level projects. You'll already have many of the supplies around the house. If not, your local craft store will be able to supply everything you need.

- Order standard invitations. Use a heart-shaped hole punch to punch cut-outs, then string through dressy ribbon in wedding colors. Or use ribbon to attach an object cast in handmade paper, a heart for example (see illustration). (A variety of paper molds are available in your local craft store.) A wallpaper backdrop or border could also be added to pre-printed invitations. Charms, pearls, and ribbon flowers are other crowning touches.

- Stencil a design onto invitation envelopes.

- Scent invitations or stationery. One method calls for filling a square sachet of cheese-cloth or muslin with your favorite potpourri. Place the sachet in a sealed container with your stationery for one month. Another method calls for putting a piece of blotter paper at the bottom of a stationery box. Add drops of your favorite oil scent to the paper. Place stationery in the box and seal for several weeks. Scented flower petals can be a refreshing addition to envelopes.

- Decorate invitation envelopes with rubber stamps. Color or emboss them to add extra dimension.

- Make your own paper to create eye-catching invitations, note cards, wrapping paper, and journal covers. Handmade paper kits which feature simple instructions are wide-ly available. Call Paper Journey at (800) 827-2737 for more information. When making paper, add a variety of herbs or flower petals to the mix and highlight the symbolism behind those that you've chosen on the invitation. (Our ancestors developed an unspoken language for flowers, giving each its own meaning. You may want to include a chart that spotlights some of these examples on your invitation. A brief chart is given on pages 71–72.) For instance, you can add rosemary which means "remembrance" to your bridal shower thank-you notes and a sentiment such as "I'll always remember your thoughtfulness."

- Hole punch basic place cards and string through raffia, ribbon, shells, charms, or buttons.

- For a casual prewedding festivity, turn paper plates into anything from beach balls to balloons. All it takes is a little imagination and simple notions.

    To make a balloon paper plate, for example: Glue a small cone made of paper to the back side of the plate's rim. Tie a piece of string to the cone (see illustration).

- Design your own luminaries. Cut snowflakes, hearts, or other shapes onto brown paper bags. Add sand and votive candles.

- Create ice votive candle holders.

    To make: Freeze water in five gallon buckets, or on a smaller scale in butter tubs. Dump block of ice from container. Pour hot water at center of ice block to form a hole into which you can set a candle. Place ice votives along sidewalk or steps.

- Add studs and decorative gems to pillar candles in your wedding colors.

- Outline your sidewalk with terra cotta candle holders (see illustration).

    To make: Use Liquid Nails to attach small terra cotta pots to dowel rods. (A 2½-inch pot works nicely with a ⅝-inch dowel rod.) After the pot has firmly adhered to the rod, you can spray paint it in gold or your wedding colors. Finally, put a candle in the pot, add a decorative bow, and stick the rod in the ground to light the way.

- Make your own candles for decorations or favors. Drop flowers or shells into the wax to match your wedding decor. Or pour wax into oyster shells. Add citronella to keep the bugs away. Create your own unity candle or a memory candle to burn throughout the reception. Add markings for each year and use on anniversaries.

- Make your own tablecloths. Choose solid or floral patterns to meet your specific decorating needs. Chair-back slip covers or chair bows can be made from a coordinating fabric. A tapestry runner might also be an elegant addition to your buffet table.

🌺 Make bows to use on wreaths, pew decorations, or presents. You will need the following:

> *ribbon (For a seven-inch diameter bow that has seven 3¹/₂-inch loops and seven-inch tails, you will need approximately two yards of ribbon. Ribbon which has some body works best. Try wire-edged.) • thin coated wire • wire cutters • scissors • bow adornments and glue (optional)*

To make: Start by leaving desired tail length before pinching ribbon between thumb and index finger. Take ribbon up and back down to form a loop. Pinch tightly between thumb and index finger. Twist ribbon, keeping right side of ribbon outside, then take ribbon down and back up to form another even loop. Continue to make desired number of loops. Pinch and twist the ribbon between each loop. The key to a beautiful bow is keeping a tight center. Once loops are finished, cut ribbon to leave equal tail lengths. Secure loops at center with wire. Shape bow by fluffing and twisting loops into desired shape. Glue a ribbon loop around bow center or adorn with acorns, tassels, buttons, or pearls.

🌺 Grow your own flowers or plants for decorating purposes or as take-home favors for guests.

🌺 For the marrying soccer fan, use soccer balls for table centerpieces. Cut out a square from the ball, add rocks and water, then fill with a casual bouquet.

🌺 Jazz up ordinary clay pots by gluing green sheet moss to the outside. Tie with a raffia bow and fill with flowers or a votive candle.

🌺 Decorate vine wreaths with small terra cotta pots. To secure the pot to the wreath, thread wire through the drain hole at the bottom of the pot. Insert and twist the piece of wire holding the pot onto the vine. Fill pots with moss, nuts, and berries.

🏵 Construct tabletop topiaries. You will need the following:

terra cotta pots • bag of green sheet moss • topiary forms (You can make your own form by placing some foam in a pot, then add a stick with a ball of Styrofoam on top. To achieve balance, the recommended stick length is double the size of your pot, plus two inches. For instance, a six-inch pot would call for a 14-inch stick.) • glue gun • glue sticks • decorative items including an assortment of flowers and charms

To make: Insert topiary form into terra cotta pot. Use glue to cover topiary form with sheet moss. Continue decorating by adding flower and charm embellishments with glue gun. Sprigs of flowers can be clipped and used separately. Petals from flowers can also be pulled apart to get more mileage from decorations. Clay pot can be painted for further adornment. A straw wreath or heart can also serve as a topiary form. In lieu of sheet moss, you can use boxwood, Spanish moss, or wood shavings for form covering. Dried miniature rosebuds, fruit, pinecones, and ribbons are other embellishing options.

🏵 To bring the Midas touch to your buffet table decorations, spray paint an assortment of fruit with gold acrylic paint.

🏵 Create a unique container for flowers or silverware.

To make: Line up stalks of fresh asparagus around a glass cylinder or jelly jar. Secure the asparagus with a rubber band. Camouflage the rubber band with strands of raffia tied in a bow. Use clumps of sheet moss to fill in any gaps. You may substitute twigs for asparagus.

🏵 Use the core of a paper towel roll to make napkin rings. Slice the core to make several rings. Wrap individual rings with ribbon. Add adornments such as flowers, charms, bows, or chili peppers.

- Tie anything from flower stems to feathers onto napkins using raffia, ribbon, or ivy.

- Serve lemonade or iced tea from a decorative bottle with an attached decorative ice ring.

   To make: Cut off the top of a milk carton. Place the decorative bottle in the carton and fill the remaining space around the bottle with water. Stuff plentiful amounts of mint leaves and lemon wedges into the water. Use twine to keep the empty bottle in place in the carton. Put in the freezer overnight. Once frozen, cut away the carton and what's left should be a bottle surrounded by a ring of ice.

- Design a flower pen for your guest book.

   To make: Cut a silk flower stem to be the same length as an ink pen. Line up flower stem to pen so that the flower bloom is resting at the top of the pen. Attach flower stem to pen with self-adhering green floral tape, covering the entire length of the pen to make it appear as if a stem. Place pens in a vase next to guest book.

- Wrap presents which look like wedding cakes.

   To make: Wrap bridesmaids' gifts, for example, in white wrapping paper. Glue on an assortment of paper lace doilies. Top package with a bride and groom statue. Scour flea markets to find interesting and inexpensive options.

- Design your own gift wrap for bridal party presents.

   To make: Start with a roll of brown kraft paper. The reverse side of a brown grocery bag will work in a pinch and makes for good practice material. Put a small amount of paint on a paper plate. Dip one side of any sponge shape into paint and then press the paint-coated side of the sponge onto paper. The same technique can be used on note cards or napkins.

🌸 Make potpourri sachets by filling small squares of netting with potpourri. Tie together with ribbon in wedding colors.

🌸 Assemble rosebud-on-a-stem favors. You will need the following:

> *medium weight wire • wire cutters • satin material in wedding colors • tape measure • scissors • sewing machine or needle and thread (same color as material) • silk flower leaves • self-adhering green floral tape • birdseed or potpourri*

> **To make:** Start with an 18-inch piece of wire. Bend the piece of wire in half to form a sturdy stem for the flower. Cut a piece of satin material into a 5-by-5-inch square. Fold the square in half with the right sides of the material facing each other. Sew a small seam down the side to form a casing. Turn the casing right side out. Pinch the casing together at the bottom and insert wire flower stem. Attach the casing to the stem with green floral tape. Continue using the floral tape to cover the entire wire flower stem and to attach a green silk leaf. Fill the casing with birdseed or potpourri and tuck the top edges in.

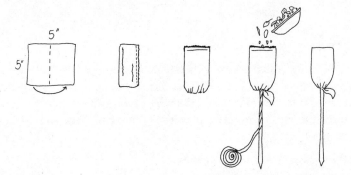

🌸 Make paper ice-cream cones to hold candy or ammunition such as birdseed or flower petals for the bride and groom's departure.

> **To make:** Roll paper of card stock weight into a cone shape and secure with a decorative seal. Fill with goodies.

🌸 Give each guest an English cracker. They can be used as take-home favors or place cards.

> **To make:** Place wedding trinkets such as rings and mints inside a cardboard tube. (The core from a roll of toilet paper works perfectly.) Roll wrapping paper

around length of tube, leaving a three inch fringe of paper on either end. Secure seam with tape. Twist excess paper at either end of cracker to form a closing. Adorn twisted ends with ribbon. Add a label with your names and wedding date.

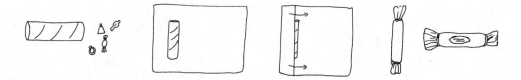

🌢 Start with basic white match packs. Personalize with paint pens and decorate by gluing on charms.

🌢 Make your own candy favors or monogrammed mints.

🌢 Enroll in a class at your local craft store and learn how to make centerpieces or fold napkins. Try the fan napkin fold for example.

> **To make:** Begin with an open square napkin. Fold entire napkin from bottom into accordion pleats. Bring both ends of pleated napkin together. Secure at center of napkin with ribbon. Fan out pleats.

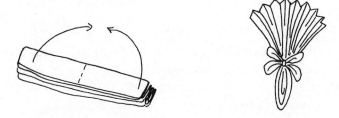

🌢 Dance the night away in little white bridal tennies.

> **To make:** Start with your basic white canvas tennis shoes. Glue on decorative lace and pearls. Replace shoestrings with fancy white ribbons.

🌢 Frame your wedding invitation in a shadow box. Add other wedding mementos or pressed flowers from your bridal bouquet or his boutonniere. Or mount your invitation in stained glass.

🌺 Make your own frames to hold favorite wedding or honeymoon photos. Start with a basic gold frame and add gold charms or buttons. To house a honeymoon memory from the beach, paint a wooden frame in a sand color and glue on seashells of different shapes and sizes.

🌺 Preserve your bridal bouquet. Simply hang it upside down in a dark, dry room to maintain the best shape. Silica sand, which is available in most craft stores, is another good means of preservation. If it dries well, you may want to display it as-is, or you could consider plucking out the best sprigs to be incorporated into a flower arrangement or wreath. The smaller flowers may be used to make potpourri. If preserving your flowers is especially important to you, with the help of your florist you can choose flowers specifically for their drying capabilities. Yarrow, hydrangeas, roses, statice, and berries such as bittersweet, buckbrush, and tallow are good choices.

🌺 Start ivy plants from sprigs used in wedding floral arrangements. (One grandmother surprised her granddaughter bride on her first anniversary with a plant she had started for her after the wedding from her reception centerpieces.)

🌺 Design your own shower or wedding thank-you notes.

> **To make:** Buy some plain, pretty linen stationery. Paste a dried flower on the front, and add the words "Thank You" in a pretty script. Scent the stationery with fragrant rose oil. (See page 51 for instructions.)

Destination Honeymoon

You don't have to head to an exotic tropical island or to a heart-shaped hot tub in the Poconos to find honeymoon paradise. Anywhere the two of you can be alone to catch your breath after the wedding madness is paradise after all. Following are some additional ways to help you capture the essence of a wonderful honeymoon.

🌺 Scatter flower petals throughout your honeymoon retreat.

🌺 Remember to pack items such as bubble bath, wine, toasting glasses, and candles for your romantic vacation. Pack a little present as an additional surprise for your groom.

🌺 Keep a journal on your honeymoon to provide years of anniversary pleasure.

🌺 Call ahead to the chamber of commerce or department of tourism to find out about local activities and festivals occurring in the area where you'll be honeymooning.

♣ Tell the resort again upon your arrival that you're honeymooning. You might just end up with a complimentary upgrade on your room or a surprise bottle of champagne. They should strive to make a good first impression so to encourage your return for future anniversary celebrations.

So the Honeymoon's Over...It Doesn't Have to Be

The whirlwind of excitement, which began when he first proposed and reached a crescendo on your wedding day, doesn't have to come to a crashing halt just because you've washed the last load of laundry from the honeymoon. Try any of our posthoneymoon suggestions.

♣ Invite both sets of parents to your new home for dinner. Watch the wedding video and share snapshots. If professional proofs are in, it would be a great time to look at those as well. Or share the same with your bridal party at a champagne reception. Don't bore them with the entire ceremony, rather just the video highlights. This can be a marvelous way to say thank you, while also giving them the opportunity to see if they closed their eyes in any photographs.

♣ Open wedding gifts with family and close friends. This can also be done immediately following the wedding if you're not leaving right away on your honeymoon.

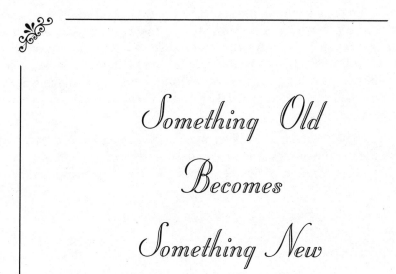

Something Old

Becomes

Something New

A Look at Forgotten Wedding Traditions

When something old is woven into something new, the end result is something special. Throughout this section you'll learn about timeless traditions you can incorporate into your special day in a variety of ways. For example, you'll learn about regard rings, age-old toasting rituals, and the symbolism Victorians assigned to different flowers. You'll also learn how many traditions took hold, such as why a bride wears the wedding ring on her third finger. Would you believe it's because in days of old a vein was thought to run from that finger directly to the heart?

For your reading enjoyment and to enhance your planning prowess, we've taken some other favorites under the microscope. As you dust off the cobwebs from a forgotten custom to use in your celebration, remember to pass along an explanation of the tradition to your guests.

How It All Began

Brides haven't always looked forward to their wedding day with great anticipation. In ancient days, they didn't coordinate and plot the ultimate affair for months upon end. Instead, in many cultures the bride of those days was literally "caught" by surprise by natives from another tribe.

This primitive groom and his comrades in many ways parallel today's groomsmen. (For a minute, picture your groom and his best friends watching a football game, and it is probably safe to say that you've seen some primitive behavior.) Nevertheless, during these somewhat barbaric times, the savage groom would generally meet with success. Despite the bride's friends' efforts to save her, the groom would carry his lady of choice away to his place of residence—just as the modern-day groom lifts his bride over the threshold. In those days, if she was lucky, she would receive a ring of braided grass to show her new "taken" status. Otherwise, it might be shackles.

The honeymoon wasn't quite as we know it today either. The groom and his new bride would hide out until the men from the bride's tribe gave up their search for their missing tribe member. The word *honeymoon* is said to derive from the fact that during this time the newlyweds would drink wine with honey, hiding out for approximately thirty days or until the moon went through all its phases.

Marriage by capture eventually evolved into marriage by purchase. Instead of stealing the bride, the groom would pay some sort of compensation to her father or the father's tribe. This compensation paid by the groom was also known as the "wed," hence the origin of the word *wedding*. In fact, some surmise this is why it is still customary for the father of the bride to "give away" his daughter.

During this same time betrothals were serious business and considered legally binding once sealed by a kiss. Betrothals eventually gave way to engagements, which brought forth marriages more closely resembling those of today.

Divination and Superstitions about Love and Marriage

Over the years, single girls have used a variety of chants and rituals in hopes of gaining insight into the man they'll someday wed.

* To determine her future husband's name, a young maiden would pare an apple in one long peel. She would then toss the peel over her shoulder and believe it to fall in the shape of her beloved's initial. (One old-timer jokes that sometimes it took a lot of apples before you got it to fall the way you wanted it to.)

* It's believed that on Halloween apples can foretell the order in which a group of people will be married. Those participating are to tie an apple to a string and then begin turning it in circles around a fire. The apple that falls first belongs to the person who will marry first. The person whose apple remains the longest will remain single.

* Another Halloween divination calls for girls to place nuts named for would-be husbands on a fire. The first to pop on the fire will also be the first to pop the question.

* A final Halloween superstition suggests a man crawl under a blackberry bush to catch a glimpse of his future mate's shadow.

* Midsummer celebrates the longest day of the year. On Midsummer's Eve, a Swedish girl should pick seven different wildflowers, then walk home silently and backwards. Upon retiring, she should place the flowers under her pillow to dream of her future mate.

* Another Midsummer divination requires a girl to pick a rose and preserve it until Christmas, when she is to wear it to church. Her future mate should appear and take it from her.

* "He loves me, he loves me not" is heard on playgrounds throughout America as little girls pluck the petals from flowers. A similar rhyme goes:

He loves me, He don't,
He'll have me, He won't,
He would if he could, But he can't.

— ·—◄●▶—· —

    With each petal, the young girl hopes that as the last one drops to the floor, the timing will be right and the words "he loves me" will indicate her true love's affections.

♣ Likewise, the following is chanted while jumping rope or counting buttons on a shirt. When you trip or run out of buttons, you will know your future mate's destiny.

Tinker, tailor,
soldier, sailor.
Rich man, poor man,
beggar man, thief.
Doctor, lawyer,
merchant, chief.

— ·—◄●▶—· —

♣ It's thought that the occupation and status of one's husband-to-be could be foretold on St. Valentine's Day. As birds are said to pick their mates for the coming year on February 14, so too it was believed that they would help their human counterparts do the same. If the first bird a girl saw on St. Valentine's Day was a gold finch, she was assured of marrying a wealthy man. A bluebird signified poverty. A blackbird foretold of marriage to a clergyman. A robin suggested a sailor, while sight of a woodpecker equaled being an old maid.

♣ Upon retiring in an unfamiliar place, a girl was to name the four corners of the bed or room after potential beaus. It's believed that when she awoke, she would be facing the corner named after the one she was to wed.

♣ A white speck on a fingernail means a new flame in one's future.

♣ Even stubbing a toe took on special meaning.

Stub your toe, kiss your thumb,
See your beau before evening comes.

— ·—◄●▶—· —

♣ Another way to gain insight might involve sniffing some pepper.

Sneeze before you eat,
See your sweetheart before you sleep.

— ·—◄●▶—· —

🦋 A young maiden wishing to determine the identity of her future mate would put a wishbone above her doorway; the first man to enter was believed to be "the one."

🦋 Single girls often would write the letters of the alphabet on slips of paper and place them face-down in a bowl of water. It was believed that the piece of paper revealing their true love's initial would turn face up and rise to the top by morning.

🦋 Lucky was the girl who found nine peas in a pod. She would promptly place it at her door and the first available man to enter would be her future husband.

🦋 The curious courting girl is advised to find a four-leaf clover and stick it in her shoe. The first man she meets will marry her. Some girls take it a step further and swallow the four-leaf clover for the best of luck.

🦋 At bedtime a girl could abide by the following poem.

Point your shoes toward the street,
Tie your garters around your feet,
Put your stockings under your head,
And you'll dream of the one you'll wed.

🦋 If you accidentally splash water or spill flour on your apron front, it's believed you'll find yourself married to a drunk.

🦋 If someone sweeps under your feet or your chair, it's said you'll never get married.

🦋 If you throw your shoe over your shoulder and it lands with the point toward the door, it's rumored you'll be married in one year.

🦋 On Easter Monday, single girls would wear one black garter and one yellow one to increase their chances for marriage by year end. A kind-hearted bride would also wear a friend's garter to help the friend find a mate.

🦋 On Christmas, an unmarried girl would go out and pick up a stack of firewood. Once inside, she would count the logs, and if there was an even number she would some-day be a bride.

🦋 A superstitious single girl will never take the last piece of bread from a plate for fear of resulting spinsterhood.

🦋 It's suggested that single girls dust cobwebs from corners because

Where cobwebs grow,
beaus won't go.

- If four people cross arms when shaking hands, there's going to be a wedding.

- To bring back a wayward lover, a girl could throw twelve pins into a fire at midnight and say the following chant.

> *It's not these pins I wish to burn,*
> *But Bobby's heart I wish to turn,*
> *May he neither sleep nor rest,*
> *Until he's granted my request.*

Courting Folklore

In the past, dating couples were often chaperoned. To better communicate with one another while under a watchful eye, unspoken languages developed around frequently used items such as gloves, fans, and postage stamps. For instance, by dropping both gloves, a woman could express her love for someone. By wearing the right glove with the thumb exposed, she would be saying "kiss me." During Victorian times, gloves were also used on valentines and as wedding favors. A gift of gloves from a suitor was a serious step toward marriage, as he was symbolically offering the girl his hand.

The fan was another means of expression. If a woman fanned herself slowly, she indicated she was married. On the contrary, she could hold the fan in her left hand and in front of her face to hint that she was desirous of someone's acquaintance. And finally, by twirling the fan in her left hand, she could inform her suitor that they were being watched, more than likely by the chaperone.

The language of the postage stamp lingers on today. By placing a stamp upside down in the left corner of an envelope, one says "I love you," whereas to do the same in the right corner sends a message of "write no more." Likewise, secret messages are often found written under stamps.

Bundling was another courting practice. This antiquated universal tradition gave permission to a would-be groom and bride to sleep together. However, an important stipulation called for them to stay dressed and under separate sheets.

The Ring

Today there's even a traditional amount of money that should be spent on wedding rings; most say the cost should be about two months' salary. If shopping for a diamond, keep in mind its value depends on its cut, clarity, color, and carat. Diamonds, as we know them today, did not become popular until the late nineteenth century upon the discovery of the diamond mines in South Africa. However, one lucky bride-to-be, Mary of Burgundy, goes on record for having received one of the very first diamond engagement rings in 1477, when Archduke Maximilian of Austria asked for her hand in marriage with such a token. Most commoners would not begin expressing their intentions with diamonds until the South African discovery made diamonds somewhat more affordable. It was not until after World War II that double-ring ceremonies gained popularity in the states.

Although the ring is generally placed on the third finger of the left hand, at other times and in other cultures it has been worn on the thumb or on the left hand during the engagement period to be moved to the right hand during the wedding ceremony. During medieval days, the ring was moved from finger to finger as the groom paid tribute to the Trinity by saying, "In the name of the Father, the Son, and the Holy Ghost." As he said "Amen," the ring came to rest on the third finger of the left hand.

There are many other superstitions surrounding this symbol of everlasting love and eternity, including one that says great misfortune will occur if the ring is dropped during the ceremony or if the ring is lost or removed at any time during one's married life. Likewise, some caution wedding rings should be made especially for the bridal pair and tried on by no other to keep the ring from absorbing someone else's ill fortune.

Some ring styles from days of old are featured.

Birthstone Rings.

These were quite popular years ago and have maintained much of their popularity today. In the past it was considered lucky to wear your fiancé's birthstone. Following is a chart of birthstones and their traditional meanings.

January - Garnet (constancy)

February - Amethyst (sincerity, also thought to keep one sober)

March - Aquamarine (courage and intelligence)

April - Diamond (innocence and purity)

May - Emerald (success in love)

June - Pearl (health and beauty)

July - Ruby (glory, prevents nightmares, and preserves chastity — in fact it's said to darken if love is not faithful)

August - Sardonyx (matrimonial happiness)

September - Sapphire (wisdom, truth, and faithfulness)

October - Opal (hope and good fortune)

November - Topaz (fidelity and cheerfulness)

December - Turquoise (harmony and prosperity)

Gimmal Rings

A gimmal ring consists of a series of separate rings that form one ring when interlocked. During the engagement period, one is worn by the bride, one by the groom, and one by a special witness. All are brought together on the wedding day to be worn as one thereafter by the bride.

Posy Rings

These rings of yesteryear were generally engraved with a special sentiment or poem, some amazingly long in length. Today, many brides and grooms opt to have their rings engraved with their initials.

Regard Rings

These featured a variety of gemstones in a setting. By placing together the first letter from the name of each gemstone, a word was revealed. The rings got their name from the very word they often spelled, "regard." In this instance, gemstones would be placed in the following order: **r**uby, **e**merald, **g**arnet, **a**methyst, **r**uby, and **d**iamond. The rings spelled a variety of sentiments, including the fiancé's name.

Keeper Rings

The keeper ring was a somewhat short-lived tradition. Welcomed by jewelry connoisseurs, the keeper ring was simply an additional band worn to "keep" the more valuable rings beneath it from falling off.

Setting the Date

When choosing your special day, there are rhymes from days gone by that you may want to read first.

> *Monday for wealth,*
> *Tuesday for health,*
> *Wednesday the best day of all.*
> *Thursday for losses,*
> *Friday for crosses,*
> *Saturday for no luck at all.*

Married when the year is new,
He'll be loving, kind, and true.
When February birds do mate,
You may wed nor dread your fate.
If you wed when March winds blow,
Joy and sorrow both you'll know.
Marry in April when you can,
Joy for maiden and for man.
Marry in the month of May,
And you'll surely rue the day.
Marry when June roses grow,
Over land and sea you'll go.
Those who in July do wed,
Must labour for their daily bread.
Whoever wed in August be,
Many a change is sure to see.
Marry in September's shine,
Your living will be rich and fine.
If in October you do marry,
Love will come, but riches tarry.
If you wed in bleak November,
Only joys will come, remember.
When December's snows fall fast,
Marry and true love will last.

A superstitious bride will set her wedding date during a time when the moon is growing fuller and her ceremony for a time when the hands on the clock are on the rise.

The White Dress

We have Queen Victoria to thank for the popularity of today's traditional all-white wedding gown, although Anne of Brittany, upon her marriage to Louis XII of France in the late fifteenth century, was the first to wear a white once-in-a-lifetime gown. Most brides from days gone by could not afford such a luxury and chose to wear their best dress as they made their way to the altar. An old rhyme helped your foresisters make their selections.

Married in white, you have chosen right,
Married in black, you will wish yourself back,
Married in red, you wish yourself dead,
Married in green, ashamed to be seen,
Married in blue, you will always be true,
Married in pearl, you will live in a whirl,
Married in yellow, ashamed of your fellow,
Married in brown, you will live out of town,
Married in pink, your spirit will sink.

Despite the poem, red is still the traditional color of a Chinese wedding dress. In fact, American brides briefly took to wearing red wedding gowns during the Revolutionary War as a sign of rebellion. Otherwise, eighteenth-century brides favored blue gowns.

According to the poem, green—like red—should be avoided because of its association with envy, fairies, and grass stains, which could indicate a premarital romp in the grass. However, green used to be the traditional color of bridal attire in Norway; black velvet was traditional in Iceland.

While some etiquette experts believe that white is an inappropriate color for the second-time bride's wedding gown, others say it's perfectly fine. They validate their belief by the fact that white is not only a symbol of innocence, but also joy.

Whatever the color choice, it seems to be a universal belief that the groom should not see his bride's wedding gown until he sees her wearing it at the altar on their wedding day.

The Accessories

An old saying that began as a rhyme has taken on great meaning when it comes to accessorizing the bride.

Something old, something new,
Something borrowed, something blue,
And a lucky sixpence in the bride's shoe.

The taking along of "something old" and "something new" symbolizes the need to create harmony which will result in happiness as a bride takes this important transitional step in life. By borrowing something from a happily married woman, the bride hopes that some of the matron's good luck may transfer to her. The "something blue" custom has biblical ties, representing constancy, purity, and fidelity. By taking along a sixpence in your shoe, you're ensuring that wealth will follow you.

"Something old" might be an item such as jewelry or a family Bible passed down to you from your mother or grandmother. The "new" is often the bridal gown. The veil is considered an especially lucky item to borrow. (On the contrary, it is considered unlucky to try on the veil before the wedding or to let someone else try it on, as she may then vie for the heart of your beloved.) For "something blue," a garter trimmed in blue can usually be found around a bride's leg. In a pinch, American brides have had to substitute a shiny new penny or dime for lack of a sixpence.

The lace wedding veil was popularized in America during Colonial times when Nellie Custis married Lawrence Lewis, an aide of President George Washington. Legend has it she chose the lace veil because he once said she looked beautiful when he saw her behind a lace curtain.

When it comes to accessories for the bridesmaids, an etiquette book from the early 1920's recalls a time when the bridesmaids wore jewelry given to them by the groom. The custom appears to stem back to the days of marriage by capture when the groom would have to pay a bribe for his bride.

$\mathcal{F}$lowers

For many years, flowers and herbs have been picked for bridal bouquets not only for their beauty and fragrance, but also for their symbolic meanings. Following are some of the most common associations.

acacia - chaste love

almond blossom - hope and indiscretion

apple blossom - preference

aster - variety

azalea - temperance

baby's breath - fertility

bay leaf - "I change but in death."

bluebell - constancy

carnation - striped/refusal, yellow/ disdain, red/ "Alas for my poor heart."

chrysanthemum - white/truth, yellow/rejected love, red/love

daffodil - regard

daisy - innocence and gentleness

dogwood - durability

fennel - strength and worthy of all praise

forget-me-not - true love and remembrance

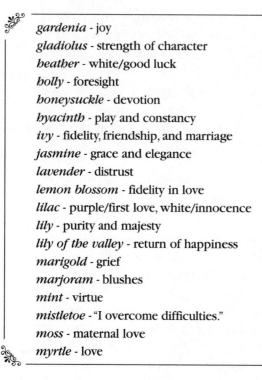

gardenia - joy

gladiolus - strength of character

heather - white/good luck

holly - foresight

honeysuckle - devotion

hyacinth - play and constancy

ivy - fidelity, friendship, and marriage

jasmine - grace and elegance

lavender - distrust

lemon blossom - fidelity in love

lilac - purple/first love, white/innocence

lily - purity and majesty

lily of the valley - return of happiness

marigold - grief

marjoram - blushes

mint - virtue

mistletoe - "I overcome difficulties."

moss - maternal love

myrtle - love

orange blossom - fertility, happiness, chastity, and "Your purity equals your loveliness."

orchid - a belle

pansy - "Think of me."

peony - shame and bashfulness

peppermint - warm feeling

phlox - agreement

rose - white/purity, yellow/jealousy, red/love

rosemary - remembrance

sage - wisdom and domestic virtue

stock - lasting beauty

sweet basil - good wishes

sweet pea - delicate pleasures

thyme - activity

tulip - yellow/hopeless love, red/declaration of love

violet - modesty and faithfulness

willow - forsaken

zinnia - thoughts of absent friends

In Victorian times, as with the regard rings, it also became popular to spell a word through the flowers chosen in your bouquet. (For example, a bouquet of **b**aby's breath, **i**vy, **l**ilies, and **l**ilacs would spell "Bill.")

Bygone bouquets were composed primarily of herbs. According to wedding lore, it was believed that the strong scent of the herbs would chase away evil spirits.

The orange blossom later grew to be the most popular wedding flower, its immense fruitfulness symbolizing fertility. These flowers were often found on veils, trains, and dresses. In more recent times the orange blossom has been replaced by stephanotis, to which it bears great resemblance. An old wives' tale indicates that the newlyweds had one month to destroy any artificial orange blossoms that were used in their wedding decor or be subject to misfortune.

Centuries ago, it was common for a bridesmaid to plant myrtle bushes at the bridal couple's new home. The myrtle would not only ensure the newlyweds' happiness, but if the bushes took root, legend foretold the single bridesmaid would soon marry. Thanks to this tradition, myrtle that was planted from Queen Victoria's bouquet in 1840 completed Princess Anne's wedding bouquet in 1973.

The bachelor's button was another flower thought capable of foretelling one's matrimonial fate. A single man would pick a bachelor's button early in the morning while the dew was still on the ground, then put it in his pocket for 24 hours. If the flower was still "true blue" the next morning, he would be happy in marriage. As bachelor's buttons are known to fade when out of water, the rite led many young men down a path of bachelorhood.

A bridesmaid's bouquet is sometimes composed of her birthday flowers. The bride's bouquet could also feature her birthday flowers or her groom's. Following is a chart of birthday flowers.

January - carnation or snowdrop	*July* - larkspur or water lily
February - violet or primrose	*August* - poppy or gladiolus
March - jonquil or violet	*September* - aster or morning glory
April - daisy or sweet pea	*October* - calendula or marigold
May - lily of the valley or hawthorn	*November* - chrysanthemum
June - rose or honeysuckle	*December* - narcissus or holly

A bouquet tied with lots of knotted ribbons is supposed to bring good fortune to the bride, as wishes are thought to be held with knots. A bridesmaid, upon catching the bride's bouquet, can increase her chances of being the next bride by making a wish as she unties one of the ribbons in the bouquet.

Toasting

It is said that the custom of toasting on special occasions began in France when a piece of toast was put at the bottom of a goblet of wine. Guests shared the wine and deemed the person who ultimately received the toast as lucky.

Another old tradition calls for the bride and groom to repeat a few lines from their wedding vows before sharing sips from a marriage cup at the reception. A Nuernberg drinking vessel, in the shape of a girl wearing a long skirt holding a cup above her head, can be used for this purpose (see illustration). The legend behind the goblet claims that a rich nobleman frowned upon his daughter's affections toward a goldsmith. He insisted that the only way the lovebirds could be together was if the goldsmith was able to design a cup from which two people could drink at the same time without spilling any wine. Much to the father's surprise, the goldsmith met with success in the Nuernberg goblet and he and the nobleman's daughter were married. To order an engravable Nuernberg goblet complete with a card explaining the legend, call the Exclusively Weddings Catalog at (800) 759-7666, Dept. BK.

In America, it is common for guests to clink their glasses throughout the wedding reception in order to keep the new bride and groom kissing. Some also believe it keeps evil spirits away.

The Cake

For centuries, the wedding cake has been an important ingredient in the recipe of wedding celebrations, and over the years many rituals have come to surround this delectable tradition. With grain serving as a symbol of fertility, biscuits were initially broken over the bride's head to ensure her fruitfulness. Guests considered the crumbs to be lucky. Biscuits were later replaced with buns piled high by guests. If the bride and groom were able to kiss over the top of the stack, they were promised many children. French chefs can take the credit for helping the buns stack better with the addition of icing. This impressive pastry evolved into today's traditional wedding cake.

It is no happenstance that the bride cuts the first slice of cake with her groom's assistance. Not only does this symbolize their willingness to share the tasks of life together, but it also increases their chances for a happy marriage and children. If the bride samples the cake before the wedding, she runs the risk of losing her husband's love. Likewise, many believe a bride should not bake her own cake.

The groom's cake has lost some ground in popularity (especially the traditional fruitcake version), but is still sometimes served in addition to the more decorative wedding or bride's cake. It is generally cut into small pieces, put in small monogrammed boxes, tied with white ribbon, and sent home with wedding guests.

To dream of her future husband, a single woman is told to pass the piece of cake through a wedding ring before putting the cake under her pillow. She's also advised to carry a piece of cake in her pocket until the newlyweds return from honeymooning so that she too might someday enjoy the same good fortune. Many couples save the top layer of their wedding cake to be eaten on their first anniversary for good luck. If it's the first wedding in a family, it is thought part of the cake should remain in the parents' house until all the girls have married. Others believe that to save a small piece of cake ensures the husband's fidelity. In some parts of the world, couples save the top cake tier for the christening of their first child.

A rendition of "The Farmer in the Dell" (in this case, referred to as "The Bride Cuts the Cake") is often played when it's time for this ritual to transpire.

The Trousseau

Trousseau derives from the French word *trousse* which means little bundle. The bride's trousseau is basically what she brings with her to the marriage, including both personal and household items. (Where Noah is said to have brought two of everything on the ark, the bride-to-be was to come even more prepared to her marriage with a dozen of everything, starched and pressed of course.) The bride who takes the time to embroider her initials onto each of the items in her trousseau is abiding by an old superstition which calls for a bride to add a stitch to each of the items in the trousseau to secure good fortune in her marriage. Superstition also dictates that items in the trousseau should not be tried on ahead of time.

According to an old Greek custom, the brothers of a family were not to marry until their sisters had each tied the knot. As such, many Greek brothers were known to help their sisters build up a hefty trousseau to increase their chances of finding a husband. In the past, the bride would invite her closest friends and family to a trousseau tea to give them an opportunity to view a display of her wedding gifts.

A Potpourri of Superstitions

Must I Really Dance in a Pig Trough?

- There was a time when the elder sisters in a family had to dance in a pig trough if their younger sister beat them to the altar. It was thought that this act would somehow help them find a husband. At minimum, it was suggested they dance barefoot at the reception.

- To be in charge of the credit cards, today's bride should pay heed to an old tradition whereby the bride would make the first purchase following the ceremony. Most often she would buy a trinket (perhaps a straight pin) from a bridesmaid to secure her future purchasing power over her husband.

- During the ceremony, the maid of honor may try to put the bride's veil over the groom's feet to make sure that the bride will be the primary decision maker in the family. An observant best man will quickly remove it on the groom's behalf.

- It's considered bad luck to walk between two people in love. If a dog comes between a couple on their wedding day, the omen is even worse.

- The adage goes, "To change the name, but not the letter means change for the worse, not for the better." In other words, it's considered bad luck if your maiden name and your husband's last name start with the same letter.

- Another rhyme, "Blest is the bride on whom the sun doth shine," sums up the preference for a sunny wedding day. Those same optimists believe that snowfall and rain will also bring good luck, but there are other schools maintaining that rain signifies the tears that lie ahead. Likewise, a windy wedding day is generally not considered a good forecast for the future. It's also believed that the weather pattern on the wedding day will give a clear indication of what the bride's life will be like. The next day's weather is said to parallel the groom's life and the following day's weather is supposed to forecast their new life together.

- On her wedding morning, the bride should jump out of bed with both feet on the floor to make sure she won't start the day on the wrong foot.

- Whoever takes the first step over the threshold of the new home will become the head of the house.

- To pour boiling water over the doorstep equals keeping the threshold warm for other members of your bridal party. By doing so, someone will get married within the next year.

- If you were a bridesmaid three times and had not yet found yourself a match, it was believed you would fail in your quest for marital bliss. The sentiment was that if you had already been showcased that many times to available men and had not yet been chosen, you were doomed to spinsterhood. However, the end of that saying, although not widely publicized, promises that if you went on to be a bridesmaid seven times, you were popular enough to break the hex.

- Some believe that leaves from the bride's bouquet have healing powers. In fact, it's said that three leaves can cure a fever.

- A public proclamation of a couple's intent to marry used to be required. Called a reading or publishing of the banns, the proclamation was made three times to give people ample time to object to the pending marriage. It was believed that the couple would run the risk of bearing deaf children if they heard the banns read.

- In lieu of a prenuptial agreement, the cautious groom could request his bride to marry barefoot. According to superstition, by marrying a barefoot person, you are ensuring you're not responsible for any of the individual's previous debts.

❧ Whoever is the first to go to bed on the wedding night is believed to be the first to die.

For Good Luck

❧ A bride often stitches a silver horseshoe attached by a satin ribbon into the hem of her bridal gown. The silver color is thought to keep uninvited guests—such as witches—away. It is also believed that the U-shape will deter evil. In fact, it should always be placed with the ends up so that good luck can't fall out. For the same reason, horseshoes are often found on cakes, bouquets, and in the groom's pocket.

❧ A bride wants to be kissed by a chimney sweep on her wedding day, as he symbolizes the home and hearth. (And we all know, home is where the "heart"h is.)

❧ For good fortune, a bride often carries salt in her pocket and avoids seeing a funeral procession on her way to the church. An empty grave in the churchyard can also prove unfortunate.

❧ The wise groom will shell out an odd rather than even amount of money for any wedding day expenditures.

❧ Many brides weep on their wedding day so that no tears will later fall in their married life. For the same reason, many also carry a handkerchief.

❧ The bridal couple should not see the car or carriage that will be transporting them turn around in front of the church or they too may have a change of heart. A car that won't start also casts bad fate.

❧ A cautious bride arranges to have a final stitch sewn on her wedding gown just before leaving for the church. This way she has not been seen in her "complete" bridal attire until the appropriate time. Along the same lines, the bride should not look at herself in a full-length mirror if completely dressed. To sneak a final peek, she can slip off a glove or shoe.

❧ When making the bridal gown, no black thread should be used for tacking. A bride is also warned not to make her own dress. A pin used to make a bride's gown is considered lucky to some and is often used in gambling. However, it's said that spinsterhood will befall the single bridesmaid who keeps a pin from a wedding dress.

❧ The bride and groom should avoid seeing one another on their wedding day until they meet at the altar. (We can probably credit the creative Victorians for this invention.)

- Go in and out the same doors, especially on your wedding day.

- At Niagara Falls, honeymooning couples heave pennies into Bridal Veil Falls while wishing for good fortune in their marriage.

- Never accept a wedding gift with a sharp point without giving the giver a coin in return or you risk severing the relationship.

Be Fruitful and Multiply

- The presence of young ring bearers and flower girls is thought to guarantee the bride's future fertility. To further perpetuate parenthood, the young flower girl carries petals, another symbol of fertility. In days of old, flower girls carried wheat.

- To symbolize fruitfulness, wheat, nuts, and rice are just some of the goodies thrown at the bride and groom. Rice, however, has become taboo as birds have been known to overindulge. A solution from Exclusively Weddings is environmentally friendly Bio Wedding Rice. Call (800) 759-7666, Dept. BK, to order.

- To increase the bride's chances of becoming a mother, the bridesmaids should lay the bride's stockings in the shape of a cross on the bridal bed.

- Within some cultures, the bride should be pregnant before the wedding to guarantee she's capable of bearing children.

If Evil Spirits Are Lurking

- Church bells often peel and car horns honk to scare away demons who may otherwise try to squelch the joyous occasion.

- The groom is warned to carry his bride over the threshold as it is considered bad luck if she trips (of course, evil spirits would be assumed the guilty culprit).

- Attendants often dress exactly like the bride and groom to fool the evil spirits and keep them from ruining wedding-day happiness. In fact, bridesmaids' attire used to include a veil. An old Roman custom called for the presence of ten witnesses or attendants. It was thought this magic number would further confuse any evil spirits.

- The veil, as a symbol of purity, is also used to shield the bride from evil spirits. A tear in the veil equals good luck.

- It is not a good idea to whistle while you wed as whistling is thought capable of summoning up evil spirits.

Old MacDonald Had a Farm

- To produce a bountiful crop of corn and herd of heifers, the farmer groom will gather a piece of every grain from the farm to put in his shoe, while the bride gathers a hair from every farm animal in hers.

- A sneeze from a cat on the day before the wedding equals good fortune for the bride.

- If you raise bees, you're supposed to go to the hive and tell them of your marriage to keep them from leaving or stinging anyone.

- On the way to the wedding, a pig in the path means turn back. An elephant, however, is a welcomed sight.

- Doubting brides may find it hard to believe that a spider crawling on a wedding gown should be a welcomed sight.

- Gray horses are considered lucky and are therefore often chosen to pull the bridal carriage.

- It's also considered good luck if a hen cackles in the bride and groom's new home.

Favors

Some of the first wedding favors were ribbons tied in love knots to be worn at the wedding and, in many cases, for days thereafter. The love knots not only represent the new union, but are also thought to bring good fortune. Snips of ribbon from the bride's bouquet or dress were often used for an extra dose of good luck. Today these favors have lost favor to many other types of departing goodies given to guests.

Shoes

Some say the tradition of tying shoes to the bumper of the newlyweds' car finds its roots in marriage by capture. As the groom escaped with his stolen bride, her father was said to throw his shoes in anger. Others believe that shoes tie into weddings as leather can be used to keep evil spirits at bay. Another popular belief links shoes to fertility, explaining why Mother Goose's "little old woman" lived in a shoe.

Historically, the exchange or throwing of shoes symbolized the completion of a bargain which, in this case, means the transfer of authority over the bride from father to groom. Accordingly, the bride's father would give the groom one of the bride's slippers.

The groom, in turn, would tap the bride over the head with it in acceptance of his new authority.

Shoes were also thrown at newlyweds to bring good luck. If the bridal pair or carriage was hit, it was considered especially good luck. If the bride throws her slipper, the one to catch it is said to be the next to marry. And finally, it is considered lucky to marry in old shoes.

Flinging the Stockings

Why does a bride toss her bouquet and the groom toss the garter? Well, it could be a preventive measure taken to keep guests from following them to the bedroom as they did in days of old. It used to be customary for guests to help the bride and groom remove their stockings, the men removing the bride's and the ladies, the groom's. The guests would then take their places at the end of the bridal couple's bed and fling the stockings over their shoulders toward the bride and groom. If a bridesmaid hit the groom with the stocking, it was said she would be the next to marry. The same holds true for the groomsman who is able to hit the bride. Later, to avoid the onslaught of single men vying for the garter which was holding up the bride's stocking, it simply became easier to toss it to the crowd.

The Bridal Shower

This tradition is believed to have direct links to the age-old dowry system. The story goes that a Dutch father so disapproved of his daughter's plans to marry a poor yet kind-hearted miller that he refused to give her a dowry. Upon hearing this, the neighbors gathered together to "shower" the couple with necessary household items.

In the 1890's another shower concept became fashionable. Gifts for the new bride were placed into a Japanese parasol. Later, the bride was "showered" with presents as the parasol was opened over her head.

A shower game from days of old involves tying all the ribbons from the opened presents together. The bride's engagement ring is attached to the last ribbon. The long strand of ribbons is then wound into a ball. Unmarried girls in attendance stand in a circle and the bride moves around the circle, unrolling the ribbon ball as she goes. When she gets to the end of the ribbon, the girl she's standing in front of will be the next to marry.

A World of Unique Ethnic Customs

You can also personalize your wedding celebration by incorporating a tradition from your or your groom's ethnic heritage. Likewise, you can introduce your wedding guests to a tradition that hales from your honeymoon destination.

One bride and groom wishing also to marry their heritages wrote in their invitations, "As we celebrate the union of our lives, so we also celebrate the joining of our heritages. We invite you to recognize and celebrate your own culture by attending in the dress of your heritage." Most of the guests respected their wish, donning everything from clogs to kilts.

Remember that dress, food, music, and decorations are some of the easiest ways to reflect a given ethnic heritage. Investigate available resources such as ethnic festivals in your area, as well as folk-dancing clubs. There may be a group of Mexican dancers or Hawaiian hula girls right in your back yard.

As you weave ethnic traditions into your special day, explain the significance of each tradition to your guests in the program or on place cards. Remember that you don't have to carry out these traditions exactly as they are written. Change them as you wish to create one-of-a-kind wedding memories for you and your guests.

To help you find just the right tradition, following is a glossary of unique wedding customs from around the world. While advanced forms of communication are allowing traditions which were once strictly tied to one culture to merge into others, this list features the traditions that are most commonly associated with various ethnic groups.

African

- In some tribes, the bride and groom's wrists are often tied together with braided grass as a celebration of marriage.

- For centuries, many African couples have been saying "I do" by jumping over a broomstick decorated with flowers to promote fertility. This act symbolically "swept" away any past quarrels and evil, giving the couple a new beginning. This tradition was brought to America by the slaves of the South. (To order a broom, see page 27.)

- Cowrie shells are often incorporated into bridal attire. The shells used to be exchanged as money in some parts of Africa, but today stand for good luck. (For tips on how to create a tablecloth trimmed with cowrie shells, turn to page 36.)

- Brightly colored *kente* cloth is woven in African heritage and wedding-day finery.

- In Nigeria, the sharing of the kola nut and palm wine between the bride and groom and their fathers symbolically links the two families. In fact, the union is not considered complete until this act has taken place. Even today, the parents of a Nigerian groom pay a "bride price" to the bride's family.

- Purple and gold are two colors associated with royal occasions, including weddings, throughout much of Africa.

- The *ankh*, the African symbol for eternal life, love, and unity, is often found on African wedding invitations (see illustration).

- The African groom may choose to wear a *kufi* cap while the bride wears elaborate braids.

- In South Africa, the bridesmaids organize a kitchen tea where, in lieu of cards, riddles are attached to every present with a clue about the gift's contents and giver.

Amish

- The Amish wedding ceremony is generally held midweek and after harvesting season.

Arabic

- The bride's hands and feet are artistically decorated with henna designs.

Australian

- Fruitcake sealed in a heavy icing is the traditional cake served at weddings down under. The hard icing actually preserves the cake so that the couple can enjoy the top tier upon the birth of their first child. The bride and groom cut the cake together but do not feed one another the first slice.

- After the toast, a special guest reads telegrams sent to the bride and groom by those who were unable to attend the wedding festivities.

- Aussies use a bridal waltz for the first dance of the bride and groom at the wedding reception.

- A "departure circle" is formed at an Australian wedding reception. As the reception draws to a close, guests are invited to form a circle. The bride and groom go in opposite directions inside the circle to bid guests farewell.

Austrian

- The Austrian bride's headpiece is usually adorned with myrtle.

- Following the wedding ceremony, recruited friends of the bridal pair wear funny hats with peacock feathers and entertain the wedding guests.

- During the bride's dance, someone steals the bride from the groom, and the bride's father has to look for her. The kidnappers will visit a number of watering holes. If the bride's father is unsuccessful in his mission, he must pick up the bar tabs that have accumulated along the way. It is also customary for him to wear a string of corks around his waist, the number of corks indicating how much was consumed before he found his daughter.

- The Austrian bridal pair literally dance out the door at midnight.

Belgian

- A handkerchief embroidered by the Belgian bride with her name or initials serves as a keepsake and is passed on to the next bride in the family.

Bermudian

- A small tree serves as the topper for the wedding cake and is later planted by the newlyweds.

Brazilian

- During youth, a collection of household goods is started for boys and girls alike. It's considered bad luck if anyone from the groom's family sees the bride's *enxoval*, or trousseau, before the wedding.

- In northeast regions of Brazil, handcrafted bridal wear and favors are very popular. The bride's dress is often made entirely from bobbin lace, and the veil is decorated with a combination of dried and porcelain flowers. A favorite favor is a miniature porcelain basket filled with small porcelain flowers. Favors are also sent to guests who were unable to attend the wedding festivities.

- Instead of carrying a pillow, the ring bearer carries an ornate treasure trunk which houses the rings.

- An elaborate processional parade to the church is often staged in which the groom is escorted to the church by his mother, while his father escorts the mother of the bride. The bride arrives last, escorted by her father.

- As part of the procession, young boys, also known as *pagens*, carry candles into the church to bring forth sunshine and faith to the bridal couple's future. Young girls, known as *damas*, serve as miniature bridesmaids.

- The bridal cake is usually a yellow and chocolate marble cake covered in a basket weave of white icing. In addition to the cake, a prune topped with coconut is a traditional hors d'oeuvre. (Its Portuguese name of *olhos de sogra* translates to "mother-in-law's eye.")

Bulgarian

- As a part of the engagement ritual, the fathers of the Bulgarian bride and groom break bread known as *pitta* and share it with guests. Each father tries to get the bigger piece of *pitta* to guarantee the bountiful crops will remain with him. Enemies of the bride and groom may feed a piece of *pitta* to both a cat and a dog to make the bridal pair get along as such.

- The wedding in Bulgaria begins when the wedding flag is raised. The stick for the flag must be cut from a living tree. The flag itself is comprised of red material for the groom and white material for the bride. Sometimes two separate flags are made. Each flag is adorned with garlands of popcorn and topped by a wedding nosegay and a golden apple.

- A procession of wedding guests follows the groom as he goes to fetch his bride. Before leaving her house, the bride kisses the hands of all those present. The wedding procession takes a different route to and from the bride's house to keep the newly married couple from divorcing.

- To ensure fruitfulness and easy labor for the bride, the bride's mother drops a raw egg down her daughter's neck.

Chinese

- Weddings are most often held during the Chinese New Year which celebrates the arrival of spring.

- Red is the traditional color of the wedding dress, candles, and invitations. White is generally reserved for funerals.

- Family members are honored during a special tea ceremony. As the bride and groom serve tea to their elders, they receive money in red envelopes.

- In order to keep away evil influences, a lion and dragon dance is often performed and the bride and groom say their wedding vows under an umbrella. Superstitious relatives of the groom have been known to put an ax at the ceremony entrance to keep the evil spirits from entering.

- A Chinese character symbolizing double happiness is almost always incorporated into Chinese wedding festivities (see illustration).

- Firecrackers are shot off to get the marriage off to a good start.

- Traditionally, sedan chairs transported Chinese brides.

- The Chinese bride often receives a pocketbook filled with gold and heirloom jewelry to save for a rainy day.

- Tradition calls for wedding revelers to go to the newlyweds' home after the wedding to ask for candy; they don't leave until they are given some.

- The Chinese groom makes every attempt to sit on his bride's dress on their wedding night so he'll always have the upper hand.

Colombian

- Fresh, rather than artificial, flowers are always used thanks to the many exotic varieties available there.

- Women attending the ceremony will try to steal the groom's boutonniere. The lucky snatcher will be the next to marry.

Croatian

- *"L'Jepa Si,"* which translates to "how beautiful you are," is a popular Croatian hymn played during special occasions, including weddings.

- *Povitica*, a nut bread, and *puhanse*, a light flaky pastry sprinkled with powdered sugar, are popular Croatian sweets often served at weddings.

❧ During the reception, guests make their way through the gift line commonly known as the *darovajte*, where they deposit their gift money envelopes in return for a shot of plum brandy.

❧ In some Croatian circles, apples are thought to symbolize love and marriage.

*C*zech

❧ The bride wears a crown of rosemary woven for her on the wedding eve.

❧ *Kolíbka* is among the many special dances performed at the wedding celebration. In this dance, the chief bridesmaid holds a plate in her arms as if it were a baby. Guests throw coins onto the plate to start a nest egg for the couple's future offspring.

❧ A decorated tree is secretly planted at the bride's gate. It is believed she will live as long as the tree.

*D*utch

❧ A young Dutch girl believes she will marry within the year if the first person she sees on her 18th birthday is a man.

❧ Instead of an engagement ring, a young man of the Netherlands would carve a pair of wooden shoes for his bride-to-be. She would save the shoes and wear them on her wedding day.

❧ Before the wedding a Netherlandic tradition brought friends of the bride and groom together for a sing-song. They would walk in pairs throughout the neighborhood singing songs. As each song ended, the next couple would start another song.

❧ At a party, the Dutch couple accepts well-wishes from guests while sitting under boughs of evergreen. The "ever"green symbolizes their "ever"lasting love for one another.

❧ The Netherlandic bridal bouquet used to be made of grains from the groom's farm. In the spring, the seeds from the bouquet would be planted in a bridal garden. When the bride became a mother, she would weave a garland from the grains for her child to wear at his christening.

❧ In the Netherlands, it was customary for the bridal party to gather two different kinds of flowers from every garden in the village for the "garland dance." During this dance guests would hold on to the garland made from the flowers while the minister led them through the village blessing the flower beds.

🌤 For four weeks before the wedding, the Netherlandic bride would wear a red wedding gown to church to notify all bachelors that she had been taken. On the day of the wedding, she would wear a black wedding dress to mourn the loss of her youth.

🌤 Engaged couples exchange rings. During the wedding ceremony, the groom places his engagement ring just above the engagement ring she's already wearing on the second finger or thumb of her right hand.

🌤 In Holland, it is believed good fortune will come to the those who marry when the tide is rising.

🌤 Girls from the Netherlands often wore *kissers*, a decorative headband. They were dubbed *kissers* as they were often used to prevent a boy from sneaking a kiss. By turning her head at the right time, a girl could give her suitor a mouthful of *kissers* instead of her cheek. If a girl was marrying rich, she would wear gold *kissers* for her wedding. Likewise, a boy would indicate the same by wearing gold buttons on his clothing.

🌤 The bride receives a Dutch marriage box, which is beautifully decorated and can be used to store small personal trousseau items.

🌤 A pine tree is planted for good luck in the newlyweds' yard.

English

🌤 Attendants are often children rather than adults.

🌤 In England, the bride leads the wedding party down a flower-covered path to the church.

🌤 The bride and groom often exit under an arch of swords. If it is not a military wedding, an arch is still made of like items that are relevant to the couple, anything from fishing poles to golf clubs.

🌤 Following the wedding ceremony in Cambridgeshire, a bride would embroider a cross on her husband's wedding smock. She would then tuck it away for him to wear again at his funeral.

♣ A superstitious English bride will throw a cake plate from an upper window. Her future happiness will be determined by the number of pieces into which it breaks. The more pieces, the merrier her married life will be. If it doesn't break, the marriage is considered ill-fated.

Filipino

♣ The Filipino bride would not dare try on her wedding gown before the wedding for fear the wedding would not take place.

♣ The bride and groom are joined by their parents during the procession. The groom's parents promise the bride's parents that their son will be faithful.

♣ The candle, veil, and cord sponsors each play a special part in the Filipino wedding ceremony. The cord is placed around the bride and groom's shoulders to symbolize the new union while the veil is placed over them to demonstrate their closeness. When lighting the wedding candles, Filipinos are careful not to blow out the flame for fear of also extinguishing life in the family. It is believed that to do so would mean the death of a family member.

♣ The tab for the Filipino wedding is picked up by the groom's parents.

French

♣ A French superstition suggests that if the bride breaks any glass before the wedding, it must be white or else it's best to call things off.

♣ Children use ribbons to symbolically block the pathway of the bride and groom on their way to be married. Together, they must overcome the challenge. Variations of this custom have gained popularity around the world.

♣ The bridal couple drinks from a *coupe de mariage*, an engraved, double-handled cup. The treasured heirloom is often passed to future generations.

♣ The traditional French wedding cake, called a *croquembouche*, appears as a stack of creme puffs coated with caramel.

♣ Guests bid on the bride's garter. She shows it off like a piece of art while her groom collects the money raised in his top hat.

- Mischievous friends of the French bridal couple often perform a *charivari*, where practical jokes accompanied by the banging of pots and pans serve to interrupt the newlyweds on their honeymoon night. For their efforts, the pranksters expect to be rewarded with French onion soup. In some parts of America this tradition lingers on. Called a shivaree, it is sometimes held upon a couple's return from their honeymoon.

- Upon leaving the church, the French couple walks down a path of laurel leaves. In Burgundy, a laurel tree decorated with ribbons is attached to the chimney of the bride's house. A bottle of brandy is broken over the tree, and a toast is made to the bride and groom. In Normandy, floral arches made from pine saplings and woven with white ribbon are traditional wedding decor.

- The number of buttons on the French bride's wedding gown is believed to equal the number of years she will live.

German

- During the engagement, both the bride and groom wear a gold ring on their left hand.

- Before the wedding, the German bride's belongings would be transported to her new home. The possessions traditionally included linens which she had been collecting since her confirmation, a cradle into which a doll had secretly been placed, and the second-best cow from her parents' farm sporting a wreath of flowers.

- In days of old, an official inviter, or *Hochzeitsbitter*, clad in the fanciest of attire and decorated in ribbons and flowers, would knock on wedding guests' doors with his walking stick to extend a personal rhyming invitation to attend the upcoming nuptial. Guests would accept by pinning a ribbon to his hat. The *Hochzeitsbitter* would generally be asked to enjoy a drink or two at each stop. It was thus questioned by some whether all the invitations were ever extended. At the actual wedding festivities, the inviter would become the toastmaster, calling each wedding guest forward so they could present their gift to the bride and groom.

- A celebration called a *Polterabend* is held on the wedding eve, and cracked dishes are broken to scare away evil spirits. Only china is used as broken glass would bring bad luck. The tradition requires that the bride and groom sweep up the mess.

- The German bride often borrows an heirloom gown and wears a wire crown decorated with tinsel, artificial flowers, pearls, ribbon, and colored stones. The bride generally rents the crown from the church. In addition to the crown, brides in a small German community called Elsdorf would, for example, wear a traditional costume of black which symbolized the peat they had to dig out so they could farm. The dress was trimmed with purple, which symbolized heather, a type of flower that was prevalent in the area, and green, which represented the land. Each community's colors were unique.

❧ To guarantee the marriage gets off on the right foot, the bride's mother would place dill and salt in her daughter's shoe.

❧ A fun-loving battle of the sexes will occur when the German groom tries to kneel on the hem of his bride's gown to demonstrate his superiority. She will hold her ground and simply respond by standing on his foot as they rise during the ceremony, although tradition calls for the bride and groom to be seated during much of the ceremony. Ornate chairs still remain for this purpose in some German-American churches today.

❧ Following the ceremony, the newlyweds throw pennies to guests for good luck.

❧ Traditional "wedding soup," or *Hochzeitssuppe,* made of beef, dumplings, and vegetables, is served to wedding guests. Up until 1900, it was common for all of the guests to eat the soup from the same large bowl.

❧ In Bavaria, the bride and groom saw a log in half at the reception to show they will share life's tasks.

❧ Before the groom would cross the threshold with his bride, a beer stein used to be thrown over the roof to prevent him from drinking too much. Once over the threshold, the German newlyweds would share a piece of bread in hopes that they would never go hungry. The bride would then head to the kitchen to salt the soup, demonstrating her domestic virtue.

❧ In modern-day Germany, guests present the couple with flower arrangements wherein gifts of money have been creatively incorporated.

$\mathcal{G}$reek

❧ To bring sweetness to her marriage, the Greek bride often hides a lump of sugar in her glove. Friends will also hide a small pair of scissors on the bride and groom to cut any bad tongues or hurtful talk between them.

- In the past, weddings were traditionally held on Sundays. The festivities surrounding the wedding celebration would start the week before with the displaying of the bride's dowry. Friends and family would come to view and throw rice and money on the dowry to wish that the bride and groom would together grow as old as the mountains. On the Friday before the wedding, two girls, both a friend of the bride and a friend of the groom, dressed in traditional attire, would extend the invitations to the wedding guests. A flower and a sweet treat wrapped in red paper would be attached to each invitation.

- On the Monday evening following the wedding, the celebration would continue at the village well. There the bride would throw coins into the well and wish for a prosperous marriage.

- In the Greek Orthodox ceremony, the groom's godfather or best man generally serves as the *koumbaros*, placing the crowns on the bridal couple's heads. These crowns, often family heirlooms, are joined together by a ribbon and symbolize the royal dignity of family life.

- For traditional reasons, the Greek groom may choose to wear a wedding band of gold, which represents the sun, while the bride wears a silver ring to represent the moon.

- *Kalamatianos* is a Greek line dance performed on special occasions such as weddings. It is led by a person holding one end of a handkerchief.

- Upon arrival to their new home, the Greek newlyweds must step on a piece of iron in the threshold to signify strength and health in their marriage. Friends of the bridal pair will smash a plate on the doorstep to demonstrate what will happen to enemies of the bride and groom.

- The best man will generally become the godfather of the couple's first born.

Hungarian

- When the Hungarian groom came to fetch his bride, he would first have to solve a series of riddles presented by the bride's father.

- Poems called "groomsmen's verses" accompany various courses of a Hungarian wedding dinner. As the courses are served, fun-loving poems about each dish are read. For instance, as the roast beef is served, the poem might detail how the bull was conquered.

- The Hungarian bride was welcomed into her new family in a variety of ways. In one region, a shovel, broom, and bucket were placed in front of her as she arrived at her new home. Picking them up meant she was not lazy. In other parts of Hungary, a bucket of water was placed in front of her. By kicking it over, she increased her chances for easy childbirth.

Indian

- Indian mates are often chosen for one another through an analysis of horoscopes by a priest. There are ten different checkpoints on which the pair may match. If at least seven are in unison, the marriage will take place. The day and time of the wedding are chosen in the same fashion.

- It is customary for the bride to wake up early and face the rising sun on her wedding day.

- The sprinkling of flower petals is an important part of the wedding ceremony in India. Elephants are sometimes used to help carry out this task.

- The Indian bride generally wears red attire with gold trim while the groom dresses in white.

- As a sign of marriage, the groom ties a gold medallion on yellow thread around his bride's neck and puts vermilion powder in her hair part. She will continue to wear both as symbols of her wedded status.

Irish

- The Claddagh ring is a true Irish tradition. The ring features two hands holding a crowned heart. The hands represent friendship, while the crown stands for loyalty, and the heart for love. When the point of the heart points toward the wearer's heart, it signifies the wearer is married.

- A fruitcake with a touch of bourbon serves as the traditional Irish wedding cake.

- A traditional Irish blessing goes as follows.

> *May the road rise up to meet you.*
> *May the wind be always at your back.*
> *May the sun shine warm on your face,*
> *The rains fall soft on your fields.*
> *And until we meet again, may the Lord*
> *Hold you in the palm of His hand.*

- The "Irish Wedding Song" is traditionally dedicated to brides and grooms.

- A popular wedding gift for the Irish bridal couple is a crystal bell. As each round of a boxing match is brought to a close with a bell, so too should the ringing of this wedding bell put an end to any disagreements between the husband and wife. Another well-received gift is a crystal bowl. Tradition foretells that as long as the bowl remains safe, the marriage will be blessed. To get your hands on either, call the Irish Crystal Company at (800) 783-4438.

*I*talian

- There was a time when a procession of the groom's family and friends would go to the bride's home where the groom's father would collect the bride for the wedding festivities. The bridal pair were then showered with wheat, bread, and salt for future fruitfulness and the procession continued on to the church.

- In post-Renaissance Venice, the best man really had his work cut out for him. He was responsible for supplying the wine and liquor for the wedding supper, giving money to the children and beggars shouting *Evviva la sposa!* or "Long live the bride" at the church door, and arranging gondolas to take the guests to the trattoria for supper.

- Today, wedding guests are given sugar-coated almonds, known as *confetti*. The sugared almonds represent the bitter and the sweet of life. *Confetti* are also used to mark other special occasions, such as births and first communions. To announce the arrival of a baby boy, for example, blue *confetti* might be wrapped in blue tulle.

- At Italian-American weddings, the bride's family members bake cookies as a sign of respect. While these cookies are shared with wedding guests at the reception, most also take home a sampling of their favorites. Traditional varieties include Italian wedding rings, fried cookies twisted into love knots, and *biscotti* covered with a sugar glaze tinted in wedding colors.

- The bride's attire generally includes a purse in which all the money envelopes can be stashed. Many guests give gifts of money in addition to wedding presents. In fact, one Italian-American bride reports she was given a strictly money shower. Another fundraising effort involves the Italian groom. In some parts of Italy, the groom snips his tie and sells pieces to guests for honeymoon spending money.

- The *tarantella* is a lively dance which is a big hit at Italian weddings. Some say the dance was originally performed to cure a tarantula bite. Others say it was the body's reaction to such a bite.

Jamaican

* In addition to a feast, a black fruitcake spiced with rum and wine and topped with white icing is served. The fruit is generally soaked in the rum and wine for a year in advance.

* For bridal portraits, rose petals are sprinkled on the bride's train.

Japanese

* In old Japan, arranged marriages were common. The parents of the bride and groom would exchange pictures and family histories to make a match. World War II, however, brought about many changes to the Japanese wedding ceremony, making it resemble, in many cases, weddings in the Western world.

* In the early twentieth century it was a common sight to see a parade of wagons carrying the bride's furniture and clothing on its way from her house to the groom's shortly before the wedding. This was done so that all could stop and admire her dowry. The bride was instructed to bring enough to last her a lifetime. A parade of the bride's dowry is a popular custom practiced in many parts of the world.

* The traditional Shinto bride is often married in a kimono bearing the groom's family crest. (This is often a gift from the groom's family to the bride at the betrothal party.) The Buddhist bride is married in a very colorful silk kimono, generally in red, gold, and silver. The kimono is adorned with cranes for good luck. The color purple is avoided in Japanese wedding attire as it is believed to fade easily and may therefore cause the couple's love to do the same.

* The Japanese couple ceremoniously exchange nine sips of *sake*, a type of wine made from rice. After the first sip, they are considered husband and wife. The Japanese ceremony is not always sealed with a kiss as it is in many other cultures.

* Rice cooked with red beans is considered lucky and enjoyed by all at the Japanese wedding reception, along with *sake*.

* In exchange for their gifts of money, Japanese wedding guests often receive elaborate gifts from the bridal couple or their families.

* A Japanese groom would never give his bride a strand of pearls as a wedding gift as they are thought to bring bad luck. Black pearls are considered an especially bad omen.

Jewish

- An old tradition called for the planting of a cedar tree upon the birth of a son and a willow tree for the birth of a daughter. When the children someday married, wood from their respective trees would be used to construct the *huppah*, the canopy under which a Jewish couple is generally married.

- The *huppah* symbolizes the couple's new home together. In ancient times it would be set up outdoors so that the couple would be assured as many children as there are stars in the sky. Today, the *huppah* can be constructed of fabric, flowers, or perhaps the *tallit*, or prayer shawl, from the groom's *bar mitzvah*. Sometimes friends are asked to hold the poles of the *huppah*.

- The *kiddush* cup used during the wedding ceremony is often a family heirloom. It can be passed down for generations and each time the bridal couple's names and wedding date can be engraved on the cup.

- According to some, the traditional breaking of the glass at the end of the Jewish wedding ceremony symbolizes such things as the destruction of the Temple, the scaring away of evil spirits, or the fragile nature of life. However, one rabbi instructs that it's the last time the groom is ever supposed to put his foot down. Light bulbs are sometimes used because they make a louder pop.

- In keeping with tradition, Jewish newlyweds sometimes retreat to a private room following the ceremony and break their day-long fast. Their ancient ancestors would have consummated the marriage at this time.

- Today's *ketubah*, or Jewish wedding contract, has become a work of art and is often displayed in the newlyweds' home.

- Dancing the *hora* at a Jewish wedding reception is a way to get everyone involved in the festivities.

- When the bride or groom is the last child in the family to marry, guests dance around the parents and honor them with crowns of flowers to the Yiddish song *"Die Mezinke Oysgegeben,"* which means "the youngest given."

- Some Jewish couples hire the traditional *badchan* to fill band breaks with songs and riddles.

(More Jewish traditions can be found on pages 137–138.)

Korean

- Geese are often part of a Korean bridal procession. They are used for symbolic reasons, as they mate for life.

- After the ceremony, the bride and groom bow to the elders of both families to show respect. The bride then sits before the elders and spreads out her skirt on which she will try to catch the money and other trinkets they throw to her. The more she catches in her skirt, the more prosperous the couple will be.

- At the wedding feast, a long buckwheat noodle is among the entrees served, symbolizing the couple's long life together.

- After the reception, the groom gives the bride a piggyback ride to their new home.

Lithuanian

- Because storks are thought to bring babies, it is customary for the Lithuanian bride's family to make her a dowry chest from a tree inhabited by storks.

- At Christmas celebrations, young girls pick straws from under the tablecloth. If a girl draws a long and slender straw, it is thought she will marry a tall, thin man. On the other hand, if she draws a short and stout straw, it is said her future groom will be of the same stature.

- A wreath of rue, the traditional flower of Lithuania, is often worn by the bride. As it represents virginity, it is removed at the wedding reception and replaced with a wimple.

- *Sadùte* is a dance tribute to the bride. Performed at the reception, the elaborately choreographed dance features the bride and her bridesmaids. The bridesmaids, each holding a rose, dance in two complete circles around the bride. The bride stands in the middle also holding a rose. The dance concludes with the symbolic blooming of a flower as the bridesmaids grasp hands and bend backward. At center, the bride raises her rose. After the dance, the bridesmaids give their flowers to the bride to form a bouquet.

- *Rezginele* is a maypole dance also done at the reception which utilizes both the bride and groom, as well as their attendants. The groom and bride stand center, holding a maypole tied with *juostas*, handwoven sashes. The attendants dance circles around the bridal pair, each holding a *juosta*. Going in opposite directions, the attendants weave their *juostas* around the pole. This pageantry symbolizes the weaving of the couple's lives together as one.

- The Lithuanian reception draws to a hilarious close with the "execution" of the matchmaker. The bride's relatives charge him with exaggerating the bridegroom's possessions. He is given the opportunity to bid his friends a final farewell. This is his cue to cover his face with soot and kiss every woman in attendance. The more he hams it up, the funnier his "execution." In the end, the bride takes pity on him and the guests hang a dummy matchmaker instead.

- After their wedding, the Lithuanian bride and groom will sometimes head for "The Hill of Crosses" in central Lithuania to place a cross in honor of their wedding on the hillside. This also represents a request for God to bless their new life together. Over the years, millions of crosses in all shapes and sizes have accumulated there, marking both happy and sad times in Lithuanians' lives.

Mexican

- Before the wedding, garlands of flowers and *cazuelas*, pots and pans made of clay, are hung above the bride-to-be's door.

- A Mexican wedding ceremony is not complete until the groom presents the bride with 13 gold coins, the number 13 representing Jesus and the 12 disciples. This gift of *arras* demonstrates the groom's willingness to provide for his bride.

- A lasso made of beads, pearls, and a cross is placed in a figure-eight around the bride and groom's shoulders by their godparents or another happily married couple during a special part of the Mexican wedding ceremony. This presentation signifies the two becoming one and reminds them they must not separate. An heirloom lasso is a cherished touch.

Native American

- From the Creek tribe of the Muskogee group, the aunts of the bride and groom would negotiate a marriage deal between the families. The girl would then be told to prepare some food, a favorite dish being boiled hominy. The boy she was to marry would then appear at her door and say that he was hungry. If the match was desirable to her, she would feed him. Otherwise she would tell him she didn't have any food today, making it clear that she didn't want to marry him. If she accepted him, he then had to provide her with a dwelling and food. Exactly one year from the day on which she had given him the hominy, the couple was considered officially married, although there was generally no ceremony.

- The bridal couple from the Navajo tribe shares a bowl of maize pudding to ceremoniously demonstrate their new union.

- Buckskin is considered the traditional bridal attire of some tribes.

- The Pawnee groom brings his saddle to the ceremony as a sign that he's bringing everything he owns to the marriage.

- A universal sign of divorce is when the bride throws all of her husband's belongings in front of the teepee.

Nicaraguan

- The groom's family wakes the bride the night before the wedding with a serenade of guitars.

- Instead of champagne, a fermented fruit juice called *chicha* is served to wedding guests.

- During the reception, the bridal couple leaves for the hut that has been erected in the middle of the wedding activities. There they consummate the marriage while guests dance around the hut until the wee hours of the morning.

Peruvian

- The wedding cake is decorated with multicolored ribbons. One ribbon has an actual diamond ring attached. Before the cake is cut and served to the guests, each of the single women pulls out a ribbon. The one who gets the ribbon with the ring will marry within the year. If a marriage doesn't take place, the bride has to throw a party in the girl's honor.

Polish

- Upon exiting the church, the Polish bride should ask for a coin from the groom to give to the choir boys. Once this ritual has taken place, it is believed that the groom will always share his wages with his bride.

- Honeymoon funds are raised through the traditional dollar dance where guests pay to dance with the bride or groom. For the honor, some may pin dollar bills to the bride's dress, while others hurl coins into a plate set out for collecting money. The aim is to break the plate. This tradition of paying to dance with the bridal couple is still played out at many American weddings, regardless of heritage.

🐾 Polish wedding guests dance the *mazurka*, a folk dance which requires couples to continually switch sides.

Polynesian

🐾 The bride's attire is made of *tapa*, a material composed of pounded bark from the paper mulberry.

🐾 In Hawaii, wedding attire generally includes seven *pikake* leis for the bride and a red sash for the groom.

Portuguese

🐾 Years ago it was common to wear a black bridal gown with lots of gold jewelry. The more gold you wore, the richer you were.

🐾 It is believed that everything in the Portuguese trousseau should be embroidered.

Puerto Rican

🐾 Tradition calls for the placing of *capias* on the dress of a bridal doll. During the reception, the bride removes these ribbon favors from the doll's dress and pins one on each of the wedding guests. The ribbons generally feature the bride and groom's names and wedding date.

Russian

🐾 At Russian betrothal parties in days of old, the bride's spindle was often set aflame to indicate her days of spinsterhood were over. The bride-to-be would then dress in mourning, recognizing the loss of her maidenhood.

🐾 In peasant marriages long ago, the procession to the bride's house was led by a man with a beer barrel. His goods would help the groom and company bribe their way through barricades which had been constructed by the bride's family. Whips were cracked on the way to the church to chase away evil spirits.

🐾 There was also a time when the father of the bride would provide his son-in-law with a new whip for keeping his new bride in line.

- Crowns are held by attendants over the bridal couple's heads in a Russian Orthodox wedding. As an indication of their new shared life, the bridal couple will share three sips of wine from the same cup during the ceremony. The service concludes with the singing of the hymn "God Grant You Many Years" three times.

- A current tradition in St. Petersburg calls for the bride and groom to lay flowers at the monuments of city founders and have their pictures taken after the registration ceremony.

- Following the wedding, the newlyweds will come home to find the windows and doors of their home sealed so as to prevent the entrance of any evil spirits.

Scandinavian

- At Christmas time, Scandinavians serve a rice pudding in which an almond has been hidden. The one who finds the almond in his or her serving is said to wed before the next Christmas.

- A Scandinavian lady is allowed to propose marriage on leap year. If a man should turn her down, he has to buy her material for a new dress, thereby making a donation to her trousseau.

- For good luck, Danes encourage a young girl to start saving her coins so that she can someday buy her own wedding shoes. According to tradition, the Swedish bride will spend her wedding evening with her shoes untied. If they slip off during the evening's activities, it is said she will experience the same ease in childbirth.

- Midsummer, often symbolized by a maypole, is a popular time of year to wed thanks to the season's association with fertility. To order a Midsummer maypole, in a perfect cake-topper size, call Scandinavia Place at (816) 461-6633.

- In Sweden, strong-smelling herb bouquets were believed to scare away trolls. The groom would often stitch an herb sprig into his wedding-day attire.

- For good fortune, the Swedish bride's father puts a silver coin into his daughter's left shoe, while her mother puts a gold coin in the right one.

- A procession of the wedding party from the church to the wedding dinner is often flanked by fiddlers and accordions.

- Birch boughs are a common component in Norwegian wedding decorations.

- Beautiful crowns adorn the heads of traditional Scandinavian brides. The Norwegian bride wears a crown of white flowers. The Swedish bride considers herself lucky if it rains on her bridal wreath.

- As a part of the traditional wedding celebration in Finland, the bride's maiden locks are cut, and she in turn wears a linen cap called a *tzepy* to signify her new married status. Capping ceremonies such as this are traditional in many European countries, as are games where the bride is blindfolded. At Finnish weddings, unmarried female guests dance around the blindfolded bride hoping she will crown them the next to wed. They sing the following song:

  "It has been. It has gone.
  Never will the bride be a maid more.
  Never will she dance with the crown again."

- At a Scandinavian wedding reception, guests clink glasses and toast the new union during the traditional *skoal*.

- A Scandinavian cake called *kransekage* is served not only at weddings, but also at other special occasions. It is comprised of various sizes of ring cakes which are stacked in the shape of a Christmas tree, gradually becoming smaller at the top. When the cake is made for anniversaries, the number of rings used to build the cake indicates the number of wedded years being celebrated.

- In Norway, *brudlaupskling*, a bread-like wedding cake, is served. Made with flour, it stems back to a time when flour was a scarce commodity and used only on special occasions. The cake is cut into squares and topped with a mixture of butter, cream, cheese, and syrup.

- It is customary for the bride to present a thick sour cream porridge to her new husband and other wedding guests while accompanied by a fiddler.

- At a Danish wedding reception, the toes of the groom's socks are cut off because Danish men are known to hide money in their socks. Snipping off the ends indicates the groom will be unable to hide money from his bride. The bride's veil is also cut into pieces and saved by the guests as wedding favors. In fact, veil cutting is a another common practice throughout many European countries.

- At the reception, if the Danish groom leaves the room, male guests will stand in line to steal a kiss from the bride. Upon the groom's return, guests rush to their seats and act as if nothing has happened.

- Legend holds that a Finnish bride would go door-to-door to collect her wedding presents in a pillowcase, accompanied by an old man wearing a top hat and carrying an umbrella. For his escorting efforts, the old man would receive a drink at each stop.

- A Scandinavian groom generally gives his bride a "morning gift," usually jewelry, the morning following the wedding. The custom continues as a part of future anniversary celebrations.

Scottish

- The Sark Toll Bridge was a favorite place for Scots and other runaways to say, "I do." The bridge is located over the River Sark, which forms a border between England and Scotland. As marriage laws were less strict in Scotland than in England, many couples eloped to Gretna Green where legend has it they were wed by the local blacksmith.

- Spring is a favorite time for weddings in Scotland as a couple receives an income tax rebate if the wedding is held before April 5th. December 31st is considered a lucky day to wed.

- The Scottish groom and his best man often wear kilts. During the ceremony, the groom may wrap the bride in his clan's tartan sash to welcome her to his family. The wedding colors can also be planned around the clan's tartan colors.

- According to a Scottish tradition, the bride can secure her future happiness at the end of the wedding ceremony by receiving her first kiss from the pastor.

- Bagpipes are the musical instruments of choice at a traditional Scottish wedding.

- Orchids and purple heather are popular flowers often found in the bride's bouquet.

- The Scottish Sword Dance or Highland Fling can top off a traditional Scottish celebration.

- Traditional Scottish drinking vessels, or *quaiches*, are given as gifts to mark special occasions. The thistle, an emblem of Scotland, is often found on toasting goblets (see illustration).

Slovak

- Single girls make small rosemary bouquets before the wedding. At the wedding, each girl finds a partner by asking to pin her bouquet on a single man's lapel.

- At the beginning of the reception, the Slovak couple is welcomed by the manager of the restaurant with a tray of bread and salt, symbols of hospitality. As the couple accepts the gifts, a china plate which has been hidden under the tray is dropped. The bride and groom must demonstrate how they'll cooperate with one another by cleaning up the mess. The groom sweeps as the bride holds the dustpan. Mischievous guests will kick the pieces, making it difficult to clean up.

- *Rejdová* is a dance that begins at midnight after the bride's veil is replaced by an embroidered cap. During this dance, each guest places money on a plate for a dance with the bride. The remaining guests dance in a circle around the pair. The groom must keep a watchful eye on his bride. As the dance nears its end, the groom must run into the circle and steal his bride away before someone else beats him to it and requires a ransom for her return.

Swiss

- In Switzerland, a good friend of the bride and groom acts as the *tafelmajor*, organizing amusing wedding games and shenanigans. At one lakeside wedding, the *tafelmajor* arranged to have the bride kidnapped and set out to sea on a decorated raft. The resourceful groom had to figure out a way to rescue her. In the same vein, entrances to the newlyweds' home are often barricaded. Some clever friends of one bride and groom made a pyramid of bottles filled with water which had to be removed one at a time to avoid a real mess. The *tafelmajor* has also been known to arrange other antics including sending a letter to all of the wedding guests asking them to mail a roll of toilet paper to the bride and groom on a given day. Another *tafelmajor* had each guest draw a piece of paper at the wedding with a kind deed written on it, requesting them to do things such as send a bouquet to the bride and groom on their first anniversary or baby-sit their first born on the bride's birthday. The slips of paper were treasured for years to come as were the thoughtful gestures that followed.

- If the bride and groom belong to a club or organization, fellow members will insist that the pair participate in a fun-loving game related to their hobby. For example, upon leaving the church, one scuba diving groom had to add fins, a mask, a tank, and a snorkel to his bridal attire and wade through a small pool with his bride in tow.

🕭 Long ago in certain parts of Switzerland, the groom would present the bride with a decorated pine tree, which she would in turn put in the window. On the birth of their first child, the wood from the tree would be used to make a cradle. A decorated tree is still often placed in a yard to announce the birth of a child.

Ukrainian

🕭 The festival of *Ivana Kupala* celebrates Midsummer in the Ukraine. As Midsummer is linked to fertility, so too does the festival provide a platform for single men and women to meet. One festival tradition calls for the village girls to make wreaths. Each girl then attaches her name to a wreath and throws it into a body of water. Single men swim to fetch the wreaths, and in turn, they must have dinner with the woman whose wreath they retrieved.

🕭 An egg painted with a rooster, a symbol of fertility, is a popular wedding present for Ukrainian couples. There are other customs which surround *pysanky*, or painted eggs. On Holy Saturday, the day before Easter, a single girl is to place a hand-painted egg into the basket of someone whom she would like to have as a mate. She must get the egg into his basket before the priest blesses the basket's contents. Once the basket containing the egg has been blessed, the union is considered willed by the Lord.

🕭 According to tradition, a young Ukrainian girl would accept a boy's proposal by presenting the matchmaker with a *rushnyk*, an embroidered ceremonial cloth. She could refuse the offer by presenting a pumpkin.

🕭 In lieu of a shower, a Ukrainian ritual called a *Divych vechir* brings the bridesmaids together to make head wreaths for the wedding ceremony. The wreaths are made of periwinkle, a symbol of purity and fertility. *Vinchatysia,* the old word for getting married, literally means "to get a head wreath."

🕭 A mock capture of the bride is staged during traditional Ukrainian wedding festivities. The groom must pay a ransom for her release, usually in the form of small gifts to the young kidnappers.

🕭 *Korovai*, a traditional Ukrainian wedding bread, is served to wedding guests. The bread is round and encircled by a braid of dough to symbolize the maiden's braid. To wish the couple good luck as they build their new nest together, dough birds, representing the bride and groom, and a tree of life decorate the cake. The tree of life is a branch adorned with ribbons, flowers, and periwinkle.

- A superstition surrounding the baking of the *korovai* calls for the bread to be baked at the bride's house by an uneven number of happily married women. (The magic number is usually seven.) Each of the wedding party members used to donate flour for the baking of the *korovai*, which was shared by guests to show their support of the new union.

- A *popravyny*, or repeat reception, is sometimes held for out-of-town guests and close family and friends the day after the wedding.

Vietnamese

- At a Vietnamese wedding, guests enjoy a rice dish called "Jade Hidden in the Mountain," formed from a mountain of rice covered with alternating rows of meat and vegetable toppings. The wedding celebration gets underway when one of the groomsmen removes the flower from the rice mountain's peak.

Welsh

- According to an ancient custom, a Welsh suitor would indicate his desire to court a girl by carving a wooden love spoon for her (see illustration). Some designs were elaborate and featured much symbolism. Due to this association, the word spooning became synonymous with courting and acting amorously.

  Following are some common carvings and their meanings:

  heart - I love you.

  key - You hold the keys to my heart.

  wheel - I plan to work hard for you.

  bell - Let's get married.

  links or beads - The number utilized in the spoon indicates the desired number of children.

  To order love spoons, call The Harp And Dragon at (607) 756-7372.

- The Welsh bride often takes a pin from her wedding dress and throws it over her left shoulder as insurance for a happy marriage.

- Another superstition calls for the relatives of the bride to kidnap her upon her arrival to the church. A chase then ensues by the groom and his relatives. It is believed that the one who catches the bride will wed within the year.

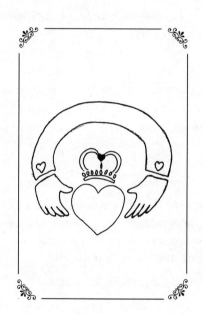

A Little

Something Extra

Checklists and Etiquette

At-a-Glance

The ABC's of Wedding Planning

Now that you're a master in creative wedding concepts, let's talk about the fundamentals of wedding planning.

When you first begin the enjoyable task of planning a wedding, the most important thing to do is break the job down into pieces. Any project can seem overwhelming when viewed in its entirety. That's where time lines can be helpful. Following is a sample time line, which can be your at-a-glance checklist, helping you track which tasks are complete and which ones remain. The sample time line provided is a blueprint on which you will need to make adaptations to fit your particular celebration. For instance, if you are planning to wed during popular wedding or holiday months, you will need to get an extra early start.

Sample Time Line

Six to Twelve Months Before the Wedding

☐ Arrange for families to meet, if they haven't already.

☐ Set budget.

☐ Decide on wedding style and level of formality.

☐ Develop guest lists. (Save them as reference for thank-you notes and Christmas cards.)

☐ Choose date and time. (Consider key participants, site availability, religious holidays, work schedules, weather, and competition from other events. You may want to call the local convention and visitors bureau to find out what else is on the calendar to make sure there will be plenty of room in the inns for your out-of-town guests.)

☐ Select officiant. (Discuss marriage classes, ceremony content, vows, video, photographs, decorations, and musical selections.)

☐ Reserve ceremony location.

☐ Reserve reception location.

☐ Have engagement picture taken.

☐ Send newspaper engagement announcements.

- [ ] Ask attendants to participate (including guest book attendant, readers, and so forth).

- [ ] Reserve hotel rooms for out-of-town guests.

- [ ] Reserve rehearsal dinner location.

- [ ] Book musicians for ceremony and reception.

- [ ] Book photographer.

- [ ] Hire caterer.

- [ ] Hire florist.

- [ ] Select wedding dress. (Inquire about alterations.)

- [ ] Choose bridesmaids dresses and schedule appropriate fittings.

- [ ] Make honeymoon reservations.(Make sure the name on your passport will match the name on your airline tickets.)

- [ ] Make postwedding housing arrangements.

Three to Six Months Before the Wedding

- [ ] Write vows.

- [ ] Confirm ceremony content.

- [ ] Secure tuxedo rentals and obtain measurements.

- [ ] Choose bridal accessories. (Find something old, new, borrowed, and blue.)

- [ ] Determine mothers' attire. (The bride's mother should call the groom's mother to discuss. Dresses should be of complementary colors and similar in length.)

- [ ] Order invitations, personal stationery, announcements, and thank-you notes. (Obtain extras for the scrapbook and mistakes.)

- [ ] Design maps.

- [ ] Meet with musicians to discuss musical selections.

- [ ] Order cake. (Look at pictures and sample. Discuss fees and delivery. Some experts suggest that the icing should match the color of the bride's gown.)

- ☐ Arrange transportation for the bridal party. (Verify in writing the year, color, and make of each car, as well as the driver's attire.)

- ☐ Complete bridal registry.

- ☐ Select wedding rings.

- ☐ Determine logistics of: reserved pews, processional and recessional, receiving line, reception room layout (including tables for gifts, cake, and place cards), parking, security (off-duty police officers are a safe bet), and coat check.

- ☐ Meet with hired professionals including caterer, florist, and photographer. (Complete any necessary paperwork.)

- ☐ Arrange necessary fittings of wedding attire.

- ☐ Plan bridesmaids' luncheon and bachelor dinner.

- ☐ Finalize rehearsal dinner details.

- ☐ Secure any rental items needed. (Your home wedding may require more rentals such as candelabra, tables, chairs, tents, altar, lighting, heating/cooling, bar equipment, stage, dance floor, audio-visual equipment, and garbage cans.)

- ☐ Send newsletter to bridal party to update.

- ☐ Secure unity candle, toasting glasses, guest book, ring pillow, flower girl basket, and cake knife.

- ☐ Shop for going-away and honeymoon attire.

- ☐ Confirm lodging arrangements for out-of-town attendants.

- ☐ Hire videographer.

- ☐ Make or order favors.

One to Two Months Before the Wedding

- ☐ Arrange final fittings of all wedding attire.

- ☐ Determine accessorizing details such as shoes, jewelry, and gloves.

- ☐ Make necessary appointments for bridal portrait, hair (schedule a trial run first), nails, and makeup.

- ☐ Address and mail invitations. (Guests should receive invitations four to six weeks prior to wedding, eight weeks in advance is appropriate for a holiday wedding. Include maps and hotel information. Make sure you've used the correct amount of postage.)

☐ Track responses and begin to coordinate seating arrangements.

☐ Address announcements.

☐ Buy gifts for groom, parents, attendants, and other special helpers.

☐ Obtain marriage license and make necessary doctor appointments.

☐ Record gifts received and thanks sent.

☐ Schedule attire pickup.

☐ Break in wedding shoes and practice bustling gown.

☐ Determine wedding-day dressing arrangements.

☐ Send wedding announcements to newspapers, including photos. (Call the society editor for specific requirements and deadlines.)

☐ Send rehearsal dinner invitations.

☐ Send bridesmaids' luncheon and bachelor dinner invitations.

☐ Finalize wedding-day agenda. (Determine the appropriate order of events including photographs, receiving line, toasts, and the serving of food, drinks, and cake.)

☐ Remind family and bridal party members of assigned wedding duties.

☐ Arrange transportation to and from the airport for out-of-town guests.

☐ Attend showers and send appropriate thanks. Bring hostess gifts.

☐ Investigate moving arrangements for transfer to new home.

The Week of the Wedding

☐ Relax.

☐ Give announcements to someone to be mailed the day after the wedding.

☐ Give caterer final count and finalize seating arrangements and place cards. (Deliver these items, along with the cake knife and toasting glasses, to caterer.)

☐ Make reminder phone calls to all hired professionals to confirm times and scheduled deliveries.

- Give wedding-day agendas to photographer, videographer, and musicians. (If the band leader will serve as emcee, provide him with names of bridal party and family for announcing, along with correct pronunciations.)

- Pack for honeymoon. (Bring address book, adapter if you're headed to another country, empty totes to carry home new purchases, and small bills for tipping. Also leave clothes in dry-cleaning bags to prevent wrinkles. Pack one change of clothes, medications, valuables, list of credit card numbers, and travel documents in your carryon luggage.)

- Prepare honeymoon itinerary for family in case of an emergency.

- Make a final checklist of things that need to be done while you're honeymooning and make necessary assignments.

- Have outdoor wedding facilities professionally sprayed with insecticide to keep away pests.

At Rehearsal

- Remind attendants of duties, give necessary equipment, and confirm dressing and photograph times.

- Give ushers a list of special guests and review seating instructions.

- Present gifts to attendants.

- Bring ribbon bouquets from bridal showers to rehearsal for practice.

The Wedding Day

- Bring maps, wedding programs, guest book, ring pillow, flower girl basket, unity candle, and favors.

- Bring an emergency kit filled with items such as needle and thread, safety pins, extra panty hose, clear nail polish, and other toiletries.

- Bring phone numbers of professionals you've hired including the organist, caterer, and band leader. Also bring contracts in case you need to settle a dispute.

- Bring your marriage license, rings, and money for clergy (a crisp new bill).

- Bring going-away outfit and accessories.

- ☐ Bring luggage if leaving right away on honeymoon. Also bring airline tickets, hotel confirmation numbers, traveler's checks, and passport.

- ☐ Wear a smile.

After the Honeymoon

- ☐ Select and order wedding photos.

- ☐ If taking husband's name, make necessary changes on documents such as social security card, driver's license, insurance policies, bank and charge accounts, subscriptions, passport, safe-deposit box, wills, and voter registration.

- ☐ Send thank-you notes.

To assist you in your planning efforts, you may want to employ the services of a bridal consultant. A consultant can prove instrumental to your success, especially if you are planning a wedding out of town. These individuals can become time-savers as well as money-savers. They are specialists at what they do and can provide not only creative but many times thrifty solutions. They bring repeat business to area vendors and therefore may get a discounted rate. Bridal consultants may charge a flat fee, a percentage of your wedding expenditures, or by the hour.

Getting Organized

Buy a wedding planner or make one yourself to keep track of your ideas as well as your contracts. Include time lines and deadlines and stick to them. Remember that there are also computer programs available to ease the record-keeping arm of your wedding plans. They can help you track everything from guest lists to thank-you notes.

Establish a file card system. To begin with, buy a recipe card holder and ruled note cards to fit inside. For each invitation sent, write out a note card complete with the guest's name, address, and phone number. Include spaces for noting their regret or acceptance of your invitation, as well as the number planning to attend. Also leave room to make notations on gifts received and thanks sent.

During your planning process, checklists will become essential. If you will be honeymooning immediately after your wedding festivities, remember to leave a postwedding checklist behind for a close relative or friend. Include items such as where to store your cake top and who will return the tuxedos.

Setting the Budget

Determine who will be financing your wedding affair. It may be the bride's family, the groom's family, the bride and groom, or a combination thereof.

Next, continue brainstorming about the type of wedding you would like to have. What have you always pictured? Remember to include input from your groom, as well as both families if they are contributing money toward your cause. Review the time line provided earlier in this chapter to ascertain what type of wedding expenses you can expect to incur. Some are associated with any type of ceremony while others grow in proportion to wedding style and size.

You may need to prioritize, choosing the items or activities you would most like to see incorporated into your celebration. After seeking bids on each line item, you will be able to see if your budget can accommodate your wishes.

It is important that you set a budget early in the ball game and stick to it. Once you know the amount of money you have available, the decision making process will be much easier. Whatever the budget you determine, rest assured that you will find a way to make most of your wedding dreams come true.

Who Pays for What

Tradition has set some guidelines, but they have become less rigid over the years. In fact, today many older brides and grooms are picking up the tab for the entire affair. The traditional way of dividing the expenses follows. (Why does tradition call for the bride's family to foot the majority of the bill? We can only guess this custom has direct ties to the dowry system.)

The bride and her family pay for

- □ All print materials and postage.
- □ All rental fees including facilities and equipment.
- □ Bride's attire, accessories, and trousseau.
- □ Groom's ring.
- □ Decorations including floral arrangements for ceremony and reception.
- □ Bridesmaids' bouquets, groom's boutonniere, and corsages for special guests.

- Wedding accessories including unity candle, guest book, wedding favors, flower girl basket, and ring pillow.
- Fee for musicians and organist at ceremony.
- Transportation for bridal party to ceremony and reception.
- Tab for reception expenses including: catering, food, cake, beverages, liquor, entertainment, security, guest parking, and gratuities.
- Wedding and engagement photographs.
- Wedding video.
- Gifts for bridesmaids and groom.
- Lodging for bride's out-of-town attendants.
- Bridesmaids' luncheon.

The groom and his family pay for

- Blood tests and marriage license.
- Officiant's fee.
- Honeymoon.
- Bride's rings.
- Groom's wedding attire.
- Gloves and ties for groom's attendants.
- Gifts for groomsmen, ushers, and bride.
- Rehearsal dinner.
- Bride's bouquet and going-away flowers, corsages for mothers and grandmothers, and boutonnieres for fathers, grandfathers, and attendants.
- Lodging for groom's out-of-town attendants.

(It has also become common for the groom's family to pay for the liquor at the reception as well as flowers for the entire wedding party.)

The attendants pay for

- Wedding attire.
- Transportation to wedding city.

It Doesn't Have to Cost a King's Ransom

You will find that you can chip away at almost any bid by doing some comparison shopping. Always make sure you're comparing apples to apples. For instance, on each catering bid clarify if gratuities and taxes are included.

Cost-Saving Measures

There are obvious ways to save even more money on your wedding expenses which include pruning your guest list, shortening the length of your celebration, or holding your ceremony and reception in the same facility. Scheduling an early or late start time to your reception will also help you avoid the need to serve an elaborate sit-down dinner. Sharing the costs with someone using the same facilities is another way to save on the bottom line. Brides getting married on the same day in the same church have been known to share floral expenses. One bride shared the expense of renting tables and chairs for her wedding reception by splitting the bill with a lady hosting an anniversary party in the same facility the night before.

To further cut your expenses, keep the season in mind. Hold your wedding off-season when bookings are light and travel off-season to your honeymoon destination when fares are lower. For your decorations, use flowers that are in-season or free-for-the-picking such as cattails and wildflowers. At your reception, serve food items that are in-season and easy to prepare. You may also limit variety.

Since liquor can be one of the larger expenses on your wedding tab, consider renting a facility that allows you to bring in your own alcohol. Keep in mind these facilities may have hidden costs if you have to import everything from the big stuff like tables, chairs, and bars to the little stuff like plenty of ice and glasses. Figuring out how much of everything you'll need will also be left on your shoulders, although most liquor stores will let you return unopened bottles. To control consumption, have food and drinks served in rounds at preestablished times. A simple wine and beer reception is another alternative.

Use credit cards for major purchases. Depending on your situation you may not only rack up frequent flyer miles, but also have recourse if a vendor's promises fall through. Ask for discounts, especially when you are buying items in bulk. Keep organized, save receipts, and copy contracts.

Investigate any family wedding heirlooms that may exist. Begin your search with old photographs. By utilizing these items in your ceremony you will not only spare expense, you'll gain nostalgia. For example, one groom proposed using the stone from his great-grandmother's wedding ring. One bride dusted off the basket her mother carried when she was a flower girl many years before.

Tips from other thrifty brides include transforming a white or ivory bridesmaid dress into a wedding gown with simple embellishments, using the bridesmaids' bouquets to form one centerpiece at the reception, incorporating a fake tier into the wedding cake, or typesetting the ceremony program on a home computer. They also suggest asking friends for favors.

The Bride Ale

As a last resort, you may want to host a bride ale instead of a wedding reception. In medieval times, the poor got married too; they just went about it a little differently. They threw bride ales (hence the word *bridal*) where guests were charged an admittance to the wedding. Lots of ale was served and the money raised paid for the festivities as well as a start-up fund for the newlyweds. A bush was posted outside the facility to welcome anyone and everyone who wanted to join the feast for a donation. Similarly, to defray the expense of a wedding in some parts of Germany, the bride's father puts a piece of burned cloth into a basket. He tells guests that the cook has burned her apron and requests that they make a donation to buy her a new one. This is an accepted way to solicit funds for a lavish celebration.

Determining Wedding Style

Nothing will influence your wedding style more than the time of day that you set for both your ceremony and reception. That time will determine the basic content of your reception as well as appropriate attire.

Generally speaking, the earlier in the day that your reception is held, the lighter the fare that accompanies it. Any celebration staged after a morning wedding or before 1 P.M. is considered a breakfast rather than a reception, even though lunch is often served. The midday affair is generally more like a brunch or tea. A late afternoon reception may serve up light hors d'oeuvres and a string quartet, while the evening reception provides either a sit-down dinner or buffet and usually a dance. Cake and champagne are included with most any celebration.

In addition to the time of day your wedding will be held, there are several factors to consider when selecting bridal attire, including the wedding style or formality, the location, the number of guests invited, the season, and the budget. Over the years, general guidelines have formed to address dressing dilemmas for a variety of wedding styles. Following are basic attire details for the formal, semiformal, and informal weddings.

Formal

The formal wedding is long on tradition. For a formal celebration the bride wears a long white or ivory gown with a longer chapel or cathedral train and a long veil. Heavily beaded gowns are saved for evening weddings. The bridesmaids and mothers also wear long gowns at a formal evening wedding, while at a daytime formal wedding shorter dresses would be appropriate. The groom, the attendants, and the fathers generally choose oxford gray or black cutaway coats, waistcoats, and striped trousers for the daytime formal wedding while an evening wedding calls for black tailcoats and matching trousers with white ties and waistcoats. The evening dress code kicks in after 6 P.M.

Semiformal

At this middle-of-the-road wedding, the bride generally chooses a floor-length gown with little or no train. That ensemble is usually complemented by a shorter veil. The bridesmaids follow suit in a length similar to that of the bride's dress. The mothers generally choose a length that is shorter by day and longer by night. For men, strollers in gray or black with striped trousers are traditional daytime attire, while a black dinner jacket or tuxedo, cummerbund, and bow tie remain the traditional evening wear. A white dinner jacket is sometimes substituted during the warmer months.

Informal

When it comes to setting the standards at the informal wedding, your taste is just as important as tradition. First, the bride's dress can be any length from short to long and anything in between. A dressy suit is also appropriate. The only rule for the bridesmaids is that they keep their skirt lengths similar to the bride's. The mothers generally wear street-length dresses. The men are also presented with a wide array of dressing options including business suits or jacket and trouser combinations. Lighter colors are generally reserved for warmer months, while a dark suit remains the staple for the cool seasons.

Tips for Working with Hired Professionals or Vendors

Begin by asking for several referrals and checking references. Try to arrange to see them in action at an event similar to your own. Carefully interview your prospective vendors, making sure that your personalities mesh. You want to like and trust them. Once everything else checks out, go with your instincts. Get everything in writing to avoid surprises, especially when it comes to fees, taxes, deposits, gratuities, escalation clauses, method of payment, overtime charges, insurance, and cancellation policies. Also get dates and times in writing.

Mark your calendar to remind you of additional payments and phone calls that need to be made. Make a note to discuss your help's attire and eating arrangements. Final reminder phone calls are always a good idea.

If friends or relatives have volunteered to perform otherwise professional duties, be especially clear and realistic about your expectations and deadlines to eliminate disappointments. If you are obtaining the services of your vendors through a hotel package plan, make sure you like the work of each individual vendor before you commit. Or check into the possibility of receiving a credit if you hire a vendor other than the one the hotel recommended.

Facilities

When choosing the facilities that will host your pending nuptial celebration, remember to take into consideration the drive time between the two facilities as well as their sizes and amenities. Make sure they will fit your needs. While you obviously want a facility that can accommodate the number of guests you want to invite, you will also want to make sure that the space is not overwhelming in comparison to the size of your guest list. With inconspicuous partitions, you can create a more cozy, friendly atmosphere for your intimate celebration. You will also want to inquire about things such as parking, restrooms, coat check, telephones, electrical outlets, heating, air conditioning, insurance, lighting, and any potential plans for renovation. In addition to discussing fees, deposits, cancellation policies, and availability, secure ample time for set up and tear down. Check to see that the location is handicapped-accessible and make sure there will be a contact person on duty at the facility while you are using it.

Additional questions for ceremony facility

☐ What are restrictions with regards to decorations, photography, and video?

☐ What equipment is available?

☐ Is the church organist available?

☐ Is there a room for the bride and bridesmaids to dress?

Additional questions for reception facility

☐ Can an outside caterer be utilized?

- [ ] Are kitchen facilities ample?
- [ ] Are the walls soundproof? What other activities will be going on at the same time, especially next door?
- [ ] Is security provided?
- [ ] Are linens, tables, and chairs included? If so, are they in good condition?
- [ ] What are additional fees if party goes over allotted time?

Discuss room layout. Consider seating arrangements, band setup, dance floor, bar and food station setup, and decorations. If you are providing the liquor, make sure you secure a liquor license.

Photography

Price and quality are two obvious factors to consider when selecting your photographer. However, it's just as important that you like the person you hire. Your photographer is one of the first people you'll interact with on your big day and you want to make sure it all gets started on the right note. Ask friends for referrals.

Pin down what's included in the package price. Ask if there can be substitutions and if proofs are included. Determine how much extra photographs will cost and if negatives can be purchased. Talk about payment plan and ordering procedures.

Review the photographer's work. Discuss your preferences, such as if you would like more captured photos rather than posed. Talk about your wish list of photo opportunities. For best results, give the photographer an outline of wedding activities. Highlight any special plans and point out important guests. Consider a combination of indoor and outdoor shots, weather permitting.

In addition to hiring a professional photographer, recruit a friend to shoot pictures at your rehearsal and rehearsal dinner. Ask her to capture exterior shots of the wedding facility, close-ups of your decorations and unity candle, candids in the dressing room, and guests arriving at the church. Do the same with video. Remember to store your photos in an acid-free album or journal.

Video

Discuss availability and cost. Also determine the length of time they plan to shoot and the number of cameras they will provide. Ask what the final package includes and if personal footage or pictures can be edited in. Also inquire about what will happen to raw footage and if that can be made available to you. And finally, prepare a suggested list of interview questions for the videographer as well as a script of events so nothing will be missed.

Discuss the videographer's position for both the ceremony and reception ahead of time. Some churches will not allow video cameras on the altar. Ask your videographer to join you for at least a few minutes at the rehearsal to eliminate any lighting complications.

Catering

You will need to decide between a cash bar and an open bar. Also discuss the cost differences of serving house brands versus premium liquors. Inquire about any corking fees which may be assessed if you bring in your own liquor and investigate liquor liability laws. Determine how and when the champagne will be dispersed.

When it comes to the food menu, weigh the benefits of a sit-down versus buffet dinner. Also discuss other serving options. For instance, determine whether guests will be served individually prepared plates or served from platters. If you go with a buffet, discuss whether places will be set and if drinks will be served by wait staff during the meal. Also discuss the special dietary needs of guests and the replenishing of buffet entrees. Likewise, determine if the cake is included in the package. Discuss cost, delivery, and serving. Determine the overall per-person cost and the final count deadline.

Other items for discussion include nonalcoholic beverages, glassware, china, silverware, serving trays, utensils, linens, tables, chairs, delivery charges, skirting, display, and staffing. If you are catering your own event, you will need ice, drink garnishments, plenty of glasses, and refrigerator space. On average, figure $1\frac{1}{2}$ drinks per person every hour. The average bottle of wine or champagne serves six, and a 16-gallon keg serves approximately two hundred.

Schedule a time for taste-testing or observe an event they've catered. When making final food selections, think about providing a variety of textures, temperatures, and colors.

Musicians

Verify the number of hours they'll play, factoring in break times. Note the number of musicians as well as their names. Discuss whether they'll play prerecorded music during breaks and accommodate special music requests. Before signing on the dotted line, make arrangements to see the band perform. Provide an agenda if you would like for the band leader to serve as your emcee.

Flowers

Provide material swatches to florist so that a perfect match can be made to your wedding colors. Discuss focal points and room layouts. For example, talk about where you and the bridal party will stand during the ceremony.

White is the traditional color for the bride's bouquet. Favorite white varieties include rose, gardenia, orchid, lily of the valley, jasmine, and stephanotis, a modern day replacement for the orange blossom. Ribbons tied with "love knots" and flowers are still popular and incorporated into many of today's bouquets. The groom's boutonniere should be a flower variety also utilized in the bride's bouquet. Bridal bouquets come in as many shapes and sizes as the brides they adorn. It is best to choose one that flatters your stature as well as your dress style. Popular bouquet shapes are the gathered nosegay, the cascade, the half-moon, and the arm bouquet. Decorated Bibles or single stems are sometimes carried in place of a bouquet.

Boutonnieres are worn on the left lapel. Corsages are worn on the left shoulder. The ribbons should be worn at the base of the corsage, not at the top, as the ribbons are primarily used to hide the mechanics. Traditionally, corsages were worn high on the shoulder so that they could be seen from the front and back.

The custom of sprinkling flower petals in the bride's path began long ago. However, because the petals can sometimes be slippery, some brides are passing on this long-standing ritual.

Ceremony Flower Checklist

- ☐ bride's bouquet (including one to toss at reception)
- ☐ altar or canopy flowers
- ☐ candelabra, candles, and decorations
- ☐ aisle runner
- ☐ pew decorations and ribbons
- ☐ guest book table decorations
- ☐ boutonnieres for groom, groomsmen, ushers, fathers, grandfathers, ring bearer, male candlelighters, clergy, and special guests or musicians
- ☐ corsages for mothers, grandmothers, female candlelighters, guest book attendant, and special guests or musicians

☐ bridesmaids' bouquets

☐ flower girl's basket/hair wreath

Reception Flower Checklist

☐ corsages for cake servers

☐ table centerpieces

☐ buffet, cake, punch, and gift table decorations

☐ dance floor decorations

☐ entrance and receiving line decorations

☐ bride's going-away corsage

Check to see that guests can carry on conversations around table centerpieces. On the same hand, if you're in a crowded room, keep decorations tall enough so they won't go unnoticed. The number of arrangements needed is directly dependent on the facilities you choose for your festivities.

Seating

Provide enough seating for what your menu demands. Finger foods can be eaten while standing, but once utensils get involved, one needs a place to sit.

At the bridal table, bride and groom take center stage. Traditionally, the best man sits to the bride's right and the maid of honor to the groom's left. The rest of the bridal party alternates boy, girl, and so forth. To include attendants' dates or mates is a welcomed gesture. The parents may have separate tables or sit together at one. The officiant and his or her spouse are asked to sit at the parents' table. If one of the bridal couple's parents are divorced, they should be seated at separate tables unless they request to sit together.

Place cards will eliminate confusion. Upon arrival to the reception, guests can be given a card with a table number. The cards are generally arranged in alphabetical order for easy retrieval. A seating diagram with the room's layout should be visible for guests to locate their table. An individual place card located by each place setting will indicate more specifically where the guest is to sit. This last minute task will take some time, so be prepared. Although the seating diagram can be drawn as soon as the room's layout has been determined, you will want to confirm actual seating assignments at the very end, due to last minute cancellations. (For superstitious reasons, the 13th table is generally deleted from seating arrangements.)

The Bridal Registry

When completing your bridal registry, you may want to explore some specialty shops in addition to department stores. Also take into account where your guests live. If a large number of them live in one city, you may also consider registering at a store in their area. Your completed registry should feature all price ranges.

If possible, avoid telling the giver you exchanged or returned a present. The same goes for the damaged present. Unless the package was insured, the giver may unfortunately feel compelled to buy you another wedding present.

If you wish to display your gifts, this is usually done in the bride's home. A white tablecloth provides a neutral backdrop. Gifts are presented unboxed. One complete place setting incorporating china, silver, and crystal pieces is usually set. If you've received more than one of any gift, only one should be displayed. Whether you include cards and checks is up to you. The amount of the check should never be made public.

In lieu of wedding gifts, you could ask that donations be made to your favorite charity. You may want to note this desire on your invitation.

Wedding Etiquette 101

Etiquette rules have been established over the years to help us navigate our way through social situations. The rules are sanctioned by society, helping to dispel confusion where it might otherwise arise. Of course, things do change over the years. For instance, in a wedding planning handbook published in 1970, respected social secretaries advised that cigarettes, "approximately two cartons of mixed brands," be put at each table in shot glasses.

Rules also vary from community to community; however, the majority of etiquette rules have an amazingly long tradition. To save you valuable time, a consensus of the etiquette experts' opinions on basic wedding traditions has been compiled.

Engagement

Parents should be told immediately of the engagement. The groom's mother should initiate a meeting of the two families if they haven't already met. Phone calls to share engagement news should be made to close friends and relatives. If you have children from a previous marriage, tell them of the engagement when you are by yourselves and in a setting that's comfortable to them. Assure them that your feelings toward them will not change.

An engagement party is generally hosted by the bride's parents. The bride's father announces the engagement by proposing a toast to the bride and groom. The groom may respond with a toast. Today's bride and groom often host their own engagement affair. Engagement parties do not require guests to bring gifts.

The engagement is announced in the newspaper shortly after the engagement party or when the wedding date is set. Each publication varies in style and deadlines, so an informational phone call should be made to the society editor well in advance.

Showers

There's not a lot to remember here, but a few standard rules have stood the test of time. The first is that friends and relatives should not be invited to more than one shower; however, moms may be the exception to the rule. The second rule is only invite to your shower those who will also be invited to your wedding. And finally, keep in mind that immediate family members of the bride or groom should never host showers for the bridal pair.

Invitations

Invitations should be mailed four to six weeks prior to your wedding. Even more lead time should be given if you are planning a holiday wedding. Invite all spouses and fiancés. Also send invitations to the bridal party and to your officiant when appropriate. You may also want to consider inviting parents of the bridal party members. When it comes to family, you generally have to draw the line somewhere. If that's the case, keep it fair. If you decide not to invite second cousins, then do so without exception to avoid hurt feelings.

Never mention where you're registered in invitations. Word of mouth will do the trick. It is also inappropriate to put "no children allowed" on invitations, even if that is your preference. The guest with any etiquette savvy should know that if the children's names are not on the inner invitation envelope, they are not invited.

The traditional formal invitation is either white, ivory, or cream and features black, raised lettering. The raised lettering is accomplished through engraving or thermography, the latter process providing the less expensive option. Invitations may be hand-written if fewer than fifty guests are invited. The bride's family's coat of arms may be used if her parents are acting as hosts. The crest should not be in color.

How to Word

Begin the process of writing your invitation copy by browsing through sample invitation books. You will find there are lots of ways to say you are getting married and that the person receiving your invitation is invited. Use "the honour of your presence" on an invitation to request attendance to your religious ceremony, and "the pleasure of your company" for a civil service or reception.

Remember that dates and times are never abbreviated. Write the time as "half after six o'clock," rather than as "half past six o'clock." The year doesn't have to be included on invitations, but if you use it, it should be spelled in full. If the wedding is held in a larger city, the address of the church should also be included. Titles such as doctor and reverend belonging to the bridal pair or hosting parents should be used if the person is ordinarily called by that title.

In the past, formal invitations used to leave a space in which guests' names would be handwritten. For example:

> *Mr. and Mrs. Tom Adams*
> *request the honour of*
> **_Mr. and Mrs. Brian Neely's_**
> *presence at the marriage of their daughter*

Today, formal invitations are worded in a variety of ways. Read on to find which example best fits your needs.

Sample Ceremony Invitations:

When bride's parents host

> *Mr. and Mrs. Tom Adams*
> *request the honour of your presence*
> *at the marriage of their daughter*
> *Julie Kay*
> *to*
> *Mr. Douglas Edward Day*
> *Saturday, the twenty-first of December*
> *at four o'clock*
> *First Baptist Church*
> *Liberty, Missouri*

When both bride and groom's parents host

—✦—

Mr. and Mrs. Tom Adams
request the honour of your presence
at the marriage of their daughter
Julie Kay
to
Mr. Douglas Edward Day
son of
Mr. and Mrs. Daniel Day

When groom's parents host

—✦—

Mr. and Mrs. Daniel Day
request the honour of your presence
at the marriage of
Miss Julie Adams
to their son
Douglas Edward Day

(In general, the groom's parents names do not appear unless they are hosting in some way.)

When bride and groom host

—✦—

The honour of your presence
is requested at the marriage of
Julie Kay Adams
to
Douglas Edward Day

When bride's parents host and bride is divorced

—✦—

Mr. and Mrs. Tom Adams
request the honour of your presence
at the marriage of their daughter
Julie Adams Baker

When bride's divorced
parents host

- - ▪▪▶ - -

> *Mrs. Kathryn Clark Adams*
> *and*
> *Mr. Tom Adams*
> *request the honour of your presence*
> *at the marriage of their daughter*
> *Julie Kay*

(Keep in mind that some etiquette experts feel that under no circumstances should divorced parents' names appear together on an invitation. Others feel that the mother's first name should be omitted, thus using only a combination of her maiden name and married surname.)

When bride's remarried
parents host

- - ▪▪▶ - -

> *Mr. and Mrs. Bill Smith*
> *and*
> *Mr. and Mrs. Tom Adams*
> *request the honour of your presence*
> *at the marriage of*
> *Julie Kay Adams*

When bride's remarried
parent hosts

- - ▪▪▶ - -

> *Mr. and Mrs. Tom Adams*
> *request the honour of your presence*
> *at the marriage of <u>his</u> daughter*
> *Julie Kay*

An easy suggestion where divorce has complicated matters

Together with their parents,
Julie Kay Adams
and
Douglas Edward Day
request the honour of your presence
at their marriage

When bride's widowed parent hosts

Mrs. Tom Adams
requests the honour of your presence
at the marriage of <u>her</u> daughter
Julie Kay

When widowed and remarried bride's mother hosts

Mr. and Mrs. Bill McIlroy
request the honour of your presence
at the marriage of <u>her</u> daughter
Julie Kay Adams

Have someone else help you proof-read all text before it goes to print. Two pairs of eyes will double your chances for proofreading success. Triple check to make sure everything is spelled correctly, that the information is factually correct, and that the day of the week and the date match up.

When all guests invited to the ceremony are also invited to the reception, one invitation containing information about both may be sent. Once information is included about the reception on the ceremony invitation, an R.S.V.P. should also be placed in the invitation's lower left hand corner.

Sample Combination Ceremony/Reception Invitation:

Mr. and Mrs. Tom Adams
request the honour of your presence
at the marriage of their daughter
Julie Kay
to
Mr. Douglas Edward Day
Saturday, the twenty-first of December
at four o'clock
First Baptist Church
Liberty, Missouri
and afterward at
Rock Hills Country Club

Kindly respond
625 Eastview Drive

By putting an address after the R.S.V.P., guests will know to send their response to your home, for instance, rather than the club where the reception is being held.

A separate reception card can be sent if you would like to invite more people to the wedding than to the reception.

Sample Reception Enclosure Card:

Reception immediately following the ceremony
Rock Hills Country Club
Kindly respond
625 Eastview Drive

If you plan to have a small wedding and then a larger reception, guests should receive an invitation to the reception and a smaller enclosure card with information about the ceremony.

Sample Reception Invitation:

> *Mr. and Mrs. Tom Adams*
> *request the pleasure of your company*
> *at the wedding reception of their daughter*
> *Julie Kay*
> *and*
> *Mr. Douglas Edward Day*
> *Saturday, the twenty-first of December*
> *at six o'clock*
> *Rock Hills Country Club*
> *Liberty, Missouri*
>
> *Kindly respond*
> *625 Eastview Drive*

Sample Ceremony Enclosure Card:

> *Ceremony at four o'clock*
> *First Baptist Church*

How to Address

All envelopes should be hand-addressed. (Sorry, computer-generated labels are too impersonal.) Two envelopes are customary; however, some modern brides are omitting the inner envelope to save money and paper.

In most circumstances, no initials or abbreviations should be used on the outer envelope. Names of streets and states should be spelled in full as well as short house numbers. The only exceptions to this rule are titles such as "Mr." and "Mrs." The outer envelope is addressed to both husband and wife, even if you only know one of them. Children's names are not included.

The inner envelope should include a title and last name of those invited such as Mr. and Mrs. Day, no addresses or first names are generally used. However, when addressing your closest relatives it's acceptable to put "Aunt Mary and Uncle Wayne," for example. If small children are also invited, the first names of the children would be listed below the parent's names. A title of "Miss" or "Mr." should be used before a teenager's name. When addressing more than one teenage girl use "Misses" and for more than one teenage boy, use "Messrs." Separate invitations should be sent to older children and adults even if they live under the same roof. The catchall phrase of "and family" is not recommended, but when a family's relations are too complex for anything else, this text may be the best solution. Although it is not necessary to include "and guest" on invitations to single individuals, if you would like for them to invite a date, this phrase may appear after their name on the inner envelope.

Order extra envelopes for mistakes. Separate inner and outer envelopes upon arrival to avoid a massive addressing boo-boo such as writing guests' full mailing addresses on inner envelopes. Arrange to get envelopes early so you may begin addressing at your leisure. Also test ink on paper to make sure it doesn't bleed through or smear.

Return addresses on outer envelopes are now considered socially acceptable and are requested by the U.S. Post Office. By providing the address, guests will also know where to send replies and gifts.

How to Stuff

All enclosures are inserted face up into the fold of the invitation. When two envelopes are used, the invitation is then placed into the inner envelope with folded edge down or with invitation copy facing envelope flap. (The tissue paper is less functional today and is used more for traditional reasons. If you use it, it should be placed directly on top of the printed copy on your invitation before envelope insertion.) The inner envelope is left unsealed and then placed into the outer envelope so that when the flap of the outer envelope is lifted, the inner envelope's front side is revealed. Thus the recipient will immediately see the names of those invited.

$\mathcal{R}$.S.V.P.

"R.S.V.P.," "the favour of a reply is requested," and "kindly respond" are all acceptable ways of requesting a response. The etiquette police hesitate to encourage the inclusion of response cards as a well-mannered guest should respond with the same formality as the invitation received. If a card is not included, here's how to respond.

Sample Acceptance

Mr. and Mrs. Bob Jones
accept with pleasure
the kind invitation of
Mr. and Mrs. Tom Adams
for
Saturday, the twenty-first of
December
at six o'clock
at Rock Hills Country Club

Sample Regret

Mr. and Mrs. Bob Jones
regret that a previous engagement
makes them unable to accept
Mr. and Mrs. Tom Adams'
kind invitation on
Saturday, the twenty-first of
December

A word of caution when it comes to leaving a blank on the response card for the number attending as you may end up with more planning to attend than were actually invited. If you use response cards, set a deadline of at least two weeks before the wedding to allow you enough time to track returns and provide a final count to the caterer. Keep in mind that many people are poor about responding, which may necessitate phone calls on your part.

Guests are not required to R.S.V.P. to a ceremony held in a house of worship. A response is necessary, however, in the case of a private residence or hotel wedding ceremony.

Maps

Include maps to all wedding festivities. They are especially helpful to out-of-town guests. Include all major roads, landmarks, and estimated miles between points. Consider putting both the ceremony and reception sites on the same map so guests can see where they are in relation to the other. Include a key to indicate which direction is north. Make directions available from a variety of starting points to accommodate all those traveling in for your wedding activities.

Pew Cards

When planning a large wedding affair, special guests are sometimes sent pew cards after they have accepted the invitation to attend (see illustration).

*Please present this card
at First Baptist Church
Saturday, the twenty-first of December*

An actual pew number and section may also be handwritten on the card. An honored guest may be invited to sit "within the ribbons," meaning the reserved sections. A pew card will help your godmother, for example, get to the right spot.

Ushering Guests In

Figure on one usher per fifty guests. The bride's guests are generally seated to the left and the groom's to the right. (The opposite holds true at some Jewish weddings.) Parents are seated in the front rows on their respective sides. (In the case of divorced parents, the mother and her new spouse, if she has remarried, are seated in the first row. However, if the child was raised by her father, then he is given front-row honors.) Strive for balance if one family has invited more guests than the other by filling in the gaps on either side. However, only special guests should be seated within the reserved pew sections. (This is where pew cards may come in handy. Guests present their card to an usher upon arrival.) No one is ushered in after the mother of the bride. At that point, the sanctuary doors are closed and late guests should seat themselves using side aisles. Pew ribbons are put in place, starting behind reserved pews, and the aisle runner is unrolled.

Ushers should arrive forty-five minutes before ceremony to seat early birds and study special seating arrangements. The usher's right arm should be offered to female guests.

Young Attendants

If you think you would like to have young attendants in your wedding, consider first their ages. Although children mature at different levels, some recommended guidelines have been set.

flower girls and ring bearers: 4–8 years of age

pages (boys or girls): slightly older than flower girls and ring bearers

junior bridesmaids and ushers: 9–14 years of age

Traditional Tunes

Discuss your musical desires with your officiant early on. Following is a list of favorite musical selections.

"Bridal Chorus" from *Lohengrin* by Wagner (otherwise known as "Here Comes the Bride")

"Wedding March" from *A Midsummer Night's Dream* by Mendelssohn

"Trumpet Voluntary" (otherwise known as "The Prince of Denmark's March") by Clarke

"Trumpet Tune" by Purcell

"Ave Maria" by Schubert

"Jesu, Joy of Man's Desiring" by Bach

"First Organ Sonata" by Mendelssohn

"The Lord's Prayer" by Malotte

"Ode to Joy" from Beethoven's *Ninth Symphony*

Canon in D by Pachelbel

"Rondeau" by Mouret

"Water Music" by Handel

"Wedding March" from *The Marriage of Figaro* by Mozart

"Toccata" from Widor's *Fifth Symphony.*

The Processional

Protestant, Catholic, or Eastern Orthodox

The groom, best man, and clergy usually enter from the front of the church, near the altar. The groomsmen or ushers begin the walk down the aisle in pairs entering from the narthex at the back of the church. Bridesmaids follow in pairs. The matron of honor, the maid of honor, the ring bearer, and the flower girl are next. (The ring bearer and flower girl may also walk in together.) Finally, the music changes, and the bride's mother stands, cueing the congregation to do the same as the bride starts her walk down the aisle. Pages or trainbearers may follow.

There are endless ways of changing the above processional to better suit your taste or needs. To begin with, bridesmaids and groomsmen may walk in single file rather than in pairs. Or they can enter as mixed pairs. All groomsmen can enter from the front with the officiant, best man, and groom. In turn, they can meet assigned bridesmaids halfway down the aisle, escorting them to the altar. Upon arriving at the altar, they can go to separate sides or as a pair to one side or the other. The processional could climax with the bride and groom entering the church together from the front or back. And finally, one could borrow from the Jewish faith and include parents and grandparents in the processional.

If a church has two aisles, the bridal party generally enters on the left and exits on the right. A general rule of thumb calls for the shortest bridal party members to begin the processional, left foot first.

Jewish

There are as many variations as there are synagogues. However, one traditional configuration calls for all participants to enter from the back of the synagogue in the following order: groomsmen, best man, groom escorted by parents, bridesmaids, maid of honor, flower girl and ring bearer, and finally, the bride with both parents.

The rabbi and grandparents may also be included in the processional. At the altar, the bride and groom stand under the *huppah*. Their parents may join in if space allows.

The Ceremony

Certain practices and beliefs are unique to each religion. Highlighted are several types of ceremonies and their distinctive traditions.

Protestant

There are many denominations under this umbrella and just as many practices, but one common denominator most agree on is a wedding blackout period during Lent. In the traditional Protestant ceremony, the bride is "given away" by her father. In today's world of equality, however, some brides are sidestepping this tradition, especially those who believe it stems back to the days when the bride was given to the groom as property in return for a bridal price of perhaps a few cows or pigs. The Protestant ceremony finds its roots in the *The Book of Common Prayer*, first published in 1549. In addition to an exchange of vows, this ceremony includes an exchange of rings.

Jewish

Within the Jewish faith, there are three denominations including Orthodox (the most traditional), Conservative, and Reform (the most liberal). In the Jewish faith, it is considered inappropriate to marry on the Sabbath (Friday sundown to Saturday sundown). Likewise, holy days are avoided. In the more traditional Jewish ceremonies, all men's heads must be covered. The marriage ceremony typically takes place under a *huppah*. The couple is often joined by the parents under this canopy. During the wedding ceremony, the Jewish bride and groom share a sip of wine from a *kiddush* cup. The ring ceremony follows. In the Orthodox wedding, the groom generally places the wedding ring on the bride's right index finger. The ring is later moved to the traditional ring finger of the left hand. The *ketubah*, or marriage contract, is presented to the bride for safekeeping. The traditional Jewish ceremony comes to a close with the breaking of the glass to cheers of *Mazel Tov* for good luck.

Catholic

In the past, banns which indicate a couple's plans to wed were either called or printed in the church bulletin for three consecutive Sundays prior to their wedding. In modern times, although the practice of the banns is far from banned, it is no longer a requirement in all churches. The bride is generally escorted by her father, though he does not verbally "give her away." Both vows and rings are usually exchanged. The Catholic wedding ceremony generally centers around a Nuptial Mass. The bride and groom are the first to receive communion. The Catholic bride and groom often present a bouquet of flowers to the Blessed Virgin Mary, as a tribute to their future plans of parenthood.

Eastern Orthodox

One of the most distinguishable features of the Eastern Orthodox wedding is the crowning of the bride and groom. Great importance is placed on the Holy Trinity in the Eastern Orthodox ceremony, explaining why rituals, such as the exchanging of the rings and crowns and the sharing of wine, are performed three times. Accordingly, when taking their first steps together as husband and wife, the priest joins the bride and groom's hands together and leads them around the altar three times while hymns are chanted.

Civil

The simplest of all is the civil ceremony as its only requirements are an officiant, a license, and witnesses.

The Recessional

Protestant, Catholic, or Eastern Orthodox

The bride and groom, as husband and wife, are the first to leave the altar. The flower girl and ring bearer follow. (The ring bearer should carry his ring pillow face down if fake rings remain.) Next, it's the maid of honor and best man. The bridesmaids and groomsmen then pair off and proceed in the same way. The officiant is last. Another option allows for the bridesmaids and groomsmen to walk separately.

Military

Basically all remains the same except that the bride and groom exit the front doors of the church under an archway of swords (navy) or sabers (army).

Jewish

The recessional begins with the bride and groom followed by the bride's parents, the groom's parents, and then attendants.

Ushering Guests Out

The ushers return after the recessional to escort the parents (bride's mother first, then groom's) and other special guests from pews. Ushers signal each row it's time to exit by removing pew ribbons. Ushers should be prepared to offer directions to the reception.

How to Receive

The correct order for the receiving line begins with the bride's mother, followed by the groom's mother, the bride, the groom, and maid of honor. Etiquette does not require fathers or bridesmaids to receive though they certainly can be included.

A final word on receiving lines is that the bride should never be congratulated. To do so would imply that she did the chasing. Instead, offer her best wishes.

The Art of Toasting

The best man should stand to propose a toast to the bride and groom at the reception and invite guests to join him. The bridal couple remains seated and does not drink as it is not proper to toast oneself. The groom in turn may propose a toast to his bride and guests. Other toasts may follow.

When preparing a toast, remember to keep it short and avoid the trite. It's also okay to be funny, but not embarrassing.

The Cake

The wedding cake can be served as dessert after the main meal or later in the reception. When cutting the cake, the groom generally puts his hand on top of the bride's to clasp the knife. A piece from the bottom layer is cut and the two feed each other a bite. In a military wedding, the groom's sword or saber is generally used to cut the cake.

May I Have This Dance?

The following dance order is generally observed, although many variations exist.

1. The bride and groom dance the first dance together.

2. The bride with her father and the groom with the bride's mother.

3. The groom's father with the bride. The groom with his mother. The bride's parents dance together.

4. The bride with the best man and the groom with the maid of honor. The remaining attendants join in. The bride's mother dances with the groom's father and the groom's mother with the bride's father.

5. Guests take to the floor.

Traditional Duties

Just as the business world is based on job descriptions, so too is the wonderful world of weddings. Certain titles bring traditional responsibilities. Read the following before making job assignments.

Best Man

- ☐ Keep the rings and officiant's fee in safekeeping. Produce at the appropriate time.

- ☐ Sign the marriage certificate.

- ☐ Propose the first toast to the bridal couple.

- ☐ Dance with the bride and the maid of honor.

- ☐ Help the bride and groom make their getaway. Guard the luggage and provide transportation to the airport if necessary.

- ☐ Supervise the return of men's formal wear.

Maid of Honor

- ☐ Host a shower for the bride-to-be.

- ☐ Hold the bride's bouquet and assist with the train during the ceremony.

- ☐ Sign the marriage certificate.

- ☐ Stand in the receiving line.

All Attendants

☐ Attend the rehearsal.

Parents of the Bridal Couple

☐ Attend the rehearsal.

☐ Mothers should plan to stand in the receiving line.

Parents of the Bride or Close Family Friends

☐ Gather the top tier of wedding cake and cake rental items, bride's gown, bouquet, guest book, cake top, and gifts. Retrieve any leftover favors, disposable cameras, and programs.

☐ Thank and pay hired professionals.

☐ Oversee return of rental items and, in some cases, unopened liquor bottles for refund. Secure deposits.

☐ Conduct any necessary cleanup.

☐ Have wedding gown cleaned and preserved.

Also Recruit Someone to Oversee the Following Assignments

☐ Check for personal belongings left behind after the ceremony.

☐ Move ceremony flowers and gifts to reception site.

☐ Coordinate place cards and seating chart at reception.

☐ Emcee reception activities.

☐ Assist photographer so candids of important people are captured.

☐ Cut the cake.

☐ Attend guest book.

☐ Hand out programs, maps, and favors.

☐ Organize bridal party by sending them down the aisle on the right foot at the right time.

At-Home Cards

Often included in wedding announcements, at-home cards inform family and friends of your new address as well as the new name you may have chosen to use.

Sample At-Home Card:

> *Mr. and Mrs. Douglas Day*
> *at home*
> *after the first of January*
> *1100 Crabcake Drive*
> *Baltimore, MD 66098*
> *(913) 555-9876*

The same information may also be stated in the wedding program.

Wedding Announcements

Sent to people who were not invited to the wedding, announcements can be a good way to share your nuptial news with professional relationships and long-time friends who live far away. Receiving a wedding announcement does not require the recipient to send a gift.

The wording of your announcement should be similar to that of your invitation, but instead of requesting the recipient's presence, you would simply substitute that you "have the honour of announcing the marriage of...." The ceremony time and name of church or synagogue are not always included, but the year is always given.

The announcements may be issued by the bride's parents, the groom's parents, or by the bride and groom.

Sample Traditional Announcement:

> *Mr. and Mrs. Tom Adams*
> *have the honour of*
> *announcing the marriage of their daughter*
> *Julie Kay*
> *to*
> *Mr. Douglas Edward Day*
> *Saturday, the twenty-first of December*
> *nineteen hundred and ninety-one*
> *Liberty, Missouri*

The announcements should be addressed like invitations and mailed the day of your wedding or the day after. Superstition dictates they should never be sent before the ceremony.

How to Say Thank You

Social secretaries vary a great deal on suggested thank-you note deadlines. An average of their recommendations indicates that you should have your thanks in a wrap two months after the wedding.

When writing notes of thanks, make your notes personal. Mention the gift by name and write as if you were talking to the giver in person. Never write as if you're just filling in the blanks. If you remember seeing the recipient at your wedding, be sure to thank him or her for attending. You might also take this opportunity to recall a special memory from the past that you share. If a large group of coworkers gave one present, then one thank-you note recognizing the group's generosity is an appropriate response. Just make sure you send it to the attention of someone responsible so it can be circulated or displayed.

Thank-you notes should be signed by the bride or groom, not both, as only one is writing the note. However, it is important that the one whose name is not signed is mentioned in the copy as appreciating the gift as well. For example, "Curtis and I would like to thank you for the gorgeous table runner...." At showers, ask someone to keep a gift list for you so that in the end you will know whom to thank for what gift.

Bridesmaids' Luncheon

The bride most often plays host to this activity, which can be held at any time. Many brides hold the luncheon early on the wedding day or schedule it to coincide with the last dress fitting.

Bachelors' Party

The groom generally hosts this party for his attendants, or the groomsmen can arrange the party on the groom's behalf. Whatever the case, a toast to the bride is always proposed by the groom. In the past, once the toast was made the glasses were then smashed so they would never be used again for any occasion of less importance. For obvious reasons, this event should not be staged the night before the wedding.

Rehearsal Dinner

This event is traditionally hosted by the groom's family on the wedding eve. The guest list for the rehearsal dinner should include the bridal couple's parents, wedding attendants and participants plus spouses or parents, clergy and spouse, as well as musicians.

You may also want to allow room for dates of single participants and out-of-town friends and relatives.

When it comes to toasting time at the rehearsal dinner, the first toast is generally offered by the host, which usually is the groom's father. From there, additional toasts may follow by the groom, the bride's father, best man, or anyone else.

Wedding Breakfast

A relative or friend may host such an event the morning of the wedding. Its primary goal is to provide breakfast for out-of-town guests. This type of activity is purely optional, as is the bridal couple's attendance.

Dissecting a Traditional Wedding Day

The start time for your ceremony will obviously have a large impact on your wedding-day time line. Following is the breakdown of a wedding day where the ceremony started at 7:00 P.M. Keep in mind it is just an example of how your wedding day activities can line up.

11:00 A.M.	Bridesmaids' luncheon.
1:00 P.M.	Bride's makeup appointment.
2:00 P.M.	Bride's hair appointment.
3:30 P.M.	Bridal party meets at church to dress. Florist has bouquets, corsages, and boutonnieres waiting.
4:15 P.M.	Bride and groom meet at altar for private time. (This couple has chosen to take all the photographs before the ceremony.)
4:30 P.M.	All posed bridal party and family pictures are taken. Caterer begins set up, the cake is delivered, and the florist puts finishing touches on buffet and cake tables. The band will set up at reception site shortly.
6:15 P.M.	Ushers assume duties.
6:30 P.M.	Prelude music begins.
6:55 P.M.	Candlelighters light candles. Grandmothers are ushered in. Mothers are ushered in (groom's first, then bride's). Ushers unroll aisle runner.

7:00 P.M.	Groom and officiant enter from vestry.
	Processional begins with Bach's "Jesu, Joy Of Man's Desiring."
	Groomsmen enter in pairs, followed by bridesmaids.
	Ring bearer and flower girl enter.
	Wagner's "Bridal Chorus" begins. The bride's mother stands, congregation follows.
	Bride walks down aisle on father's arm.
	Ceremony begins.

7:45 P.M.	Recessional begins to Mendelssohn's "Wedding March" with bride and groom leaving first, followed by children attendants, honor attendants, and bridesmaids and groomsmen in pairs.
	Mothers and other special guests are ushered out.
	Bride and groom quickly return to front of church to usher guests out.
	Parents of bridal couple receive in vestibule.

8:30 P.M.	Guests arrive at reception site after twenty minute drive.
	Background music begins.
	Waiters pass trays of champagne and hors d'oeuvres.
	(Photographs would be taken and receiving line would form if these agenda items had not already been taken care of at the church.)
	Wedding party is announced.
	Blessing.
	Best man proposes toast.
	Buffet or sit-down dinner begins.
	(To keep the pace moving, the other traditional activities can be inserted in between meal courses.)

9:30 P.M.	Cake is cut and served to guests.
	First dances begin.
	Dance floor opens to all guests.

| 10:30 P.M. | Bride throws bouquet. Garter is tossed. |
| | Bride and groom change into going-away clothes. |

| 11:00 P.M. | Bride and groom say goodbyes. Confetti is thrown as bride and groom make getaway. |

*T*hank you for letting us be a part of this special time in your life. Good luck with your wedding plans. May your day be everything you've ever dreamed it to be. As you chart your course to memorable matrimony, keep in mind that the many ideas provided in this book can be used as they are presented or customized to fit your individual needs, whatever those may be. Perhaps you'll choose to delve into the past by incorporating one of our special Victorian traditions into your wedding festivities. Or maybe you'll dive into the future by utilizing any one of the more contemporary wedding concepts we've presented. Whether it's something old or something new that you choose to weave into your wedding celebration, we hope to help you achieve something both personalized and unique. In closing, an age-old toast sums up our wishes for you and your groom.

A toast to love and laughter,

And happily ever after.

TRADITIONAL ANNIVERSARY GIFTS
(AND SOME NONTRADITIONAL INTERPRETATIONS)

first -   paper (Surprise your spouse with a tree, money, or gift certificate.)

second -   cotton (Present your honey with monogrammed cotton towels.)

third -   leather (Exchange his and hers matching watches with leather bands or slippers with leather soles.)

fourth -   silk, fruit, or flowers (Give your spouse a crate of fruit with a note that says "I'm fruity about you!" Or send flowers each month for an entire year.)

fifth -   wood (Give the gift of golf woods.)

sixth -   iron or candy (Complete the golf club set you started last year with a set of irons. Or present a box of chocolates with a note requesting a date to watch *Willy Wonka & the Chocolate Factory.*)

seventh -   copper or wool (Cuddle up in a wool stadium blanket.)

eighth -   bronze (Have something special bronzed.)

ninth -   pottery (Take a pottery class together.)

tenth -   tin or aluminum (Fill ten pie tins with your spouse's favorite kind of pie.)

eleventh -   steel ("Steal" your spouse away for a second honeymoon.)

twelfth -   linen or silk (Exchange matching silk pajamas.)

thirteenth -   lace (Enjoy a candlelight dinner on an antique lace tablecloth.)

fourteenth -   ivory (Surprise your spouse with a new piano or tickets to hear a famous pianist.)

fifteenth -   crystal (Search for a set of crystal goblets and a bottle of wine from the year you were married.)

twentieth -   china (Make Chinese fortune cookies to house fortunes such as "Take a wok on the wild side with me.")

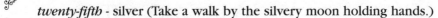

twenty-fifth - silver (Take a walk by the silvery moon holding hands.)

thirtieth -   pearl (Go out for seafood. Hide a present in an oyster.)

thirty-fifth - coral or jade (Visit the Cayman Islands for the best in black coral.)

fortieth -   ruby (Follow the Rolling Stones' lead and make up your very own "Ruby Tuesday" holiday. Celebrate each Tuesday all year long. Consider sampling a different restaurant each week.)

forty-fifth -   sapphire (Take your spouse under the deep blue sapphire sea in a submarine ride.)

fiftieth -   gold (Present your spouse with fifty pounds of gold foil-wrapped chocolate coins.)

fifty-fifth -   emerald (Welcome your spouse to Emerald City from *The Wizard of Oz*. As the "Wizard," promise to grant a different wish each week.)

sixtieth -   diamonds (Head for the ball diamond.)

Make it to seventy-five years and it's diamonds again!

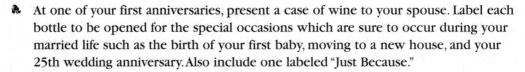

- At one of your first anniversaries, present a case of wine to your spouse. Label each bottle to be opened for the special occasions which are sure to occur during your married life such as the birth of your first baby, moving to a new house, and your 25th wedding anniversary. Also include one labeled "Just Because."

- Celebrate your love for one another each year by planting a different tree or rose bush in a garden. There's no better way to watch your love for one another grow.

- On a special anniversary, reaffirm your commitment to one another by renewing your vows in a special ceremony.

- Each New Year's Eve, make a calendar together so important dates won't be forgotten. Use stickers to flag special days throughout the coming year.

INDEX

Order Form

Quantity	Title	Author	Order No.	Unit Cost (U.S. $)	Total
	15,000+ Baby Names	Bruce Lansky	1211	$3.95	
	Best Baby Shower Book	Courtney Cooke	1239	$7.00	
	Best Baby Shower Party Game Book	Courtney Cooke	6063	$3.95	
	Best Party Book	Penny Warner	6089	$8.00	
	Best Bridal Shower Party Game Book	Courtney Cooke	6060	$3.95	
	Best Couple's Shower Party Game Book	Courtney Cooke	6061	$3.95	
	Best Wedding Shower Book	Courtney Cooke	6059	$7.00	
	Familiarity Breeds Children	Bruce Lansky	4015	$7.00	
	For Better And For Worse	Bruce Lansky	4000	$7.00	
	Joy of Friendship	Robert Scotellaro	3506	$7.00	
	Joy of Marriage	Monica/Bill Dodds	3504	$7.00	
	Joy of Sisters	Karen Brown	3508	$7.00	
	Lovesick	Bruce Lansky	4045	$7.00	
	Pick A Party	Patty Sachs	6085	$9.00	
				Subtotal	
			Shipping and Handling (see below)		
			MN residents add 6.5% sales tax		
				Total	

YES, please send me the books indicated above. Add $2.00 shipping and handling for the first book and 50¢ for each additional book. Add $2.50 to total for books shipped to Canada. Overseas postage will be billed. Allow up to four weeks for delivery. Send check or money order payable to Meadowbrook Press. No cash or C.O.D.'s please. Prices subject to change without notice. **Quantity discounts available upon request.**

Send book(s) to:

Name _____ Phone _____

Address _____

City_____ State _____ Zip _____

Payment via:

❏ Check or money order payable to Meadowbrook Press. (No cash or C.O.D.'s please) Amount enclosed $ _____

❏ Visa (for orders over $10.00 only)   ❏ MasterCard (for orders over $10.00 only)

Account #_____ Signature_____ Exp. Date _____

A FREE Meadowbrook Press catalog is available upon request.
You can also phone us for orders of $10.00 or more at 1-800-338-2232.

Mail to: Meadowbrook Press, 5451 Smetana Drive, Minnetonka, Minnesota 55343

Phone (612) 930-1100   Toll-Free 1-800-338-2232   Fax (612) 930-1940